NOON

NOON is an independent not-for-profit literary annual published by NOON, Inc.

Edition price $12.00 (domestic) or $17.00 (foreign)
All donations are tax deductible.

⟵

NOON is distributed by
Ingram Periodicals, Inc., 18 Ingram Boulevard,
La Vergne, Tennessee 37086 (800) 627-6247

NOON welcomes submissions. Send to:
Diane Williams
NOON, 1324 Lexington Avenue, PMB 298, New York, New York 10128
Please include the necessary self-addressed, stamped envelope.
We do not accept international reply coupons.
noonannual.com

NOON is indexed by *Humanities International Complete.*
Cover design by Susan Carroll, featuring *Gentleman with a Hat*, a 2015 painting
by Genieve Figgis, courtesy of the artist and Half Gallery, New York.

"A beautiful annual that remains staunchly avant-garde in its commitment to work that is oblique, enigmatic and impossible to ignore . . . stories that leave a flashbulb's glow behind the eyes even as they resist sense."

—Rachel Syme, *The New York Times,* January 15, 2016

"A compendium of unlikely pleasures: short prose and illustrations that challenge us to think about meaning and narrative. It is elegantly designed and curated, a journal that wears its intentions on its sleeve. These are oblique stories, stories that exist in the interior, getting at the things we know but do not know we know."

— David Ulin, *Los Angeles Times*

"The best stories in *NOON* are, indeed, stunning, in the sense that they leave one conscious of powerful meanings not yet fully absorbed. . . . The journal has proved its staying power and achieved a respected position. . . . *NOON* has intellectual weight. Over the years it has investigated, and pushed the boundaries of, the means and processes of communication. . . . Williams's editorial vision ensures the intelligence and integrity of the journal as a whole."

— Alison Kelly, *The Times Literary Supplement*

CONTENTS

The Editors proudly congratulate R. O. Kwon, whose story "Hey" was included in *The Best Small Fictions 2016* (Queen's Ferry Press). "Hey" appeared in the 2015 edition of NOON.

The Editors proudly congratulate Vi Khi Nao, winner of the 2016 Ronald Sukenick Innovative Fiction Contest, for *A Brief Alphabet of Torture*.

The Editors proudly congratulate Ashton Politanoff, whose story "One End and Aim" was included in *California Prose Directory 2017: New Writing from The Golden State* (Outpost 19). "One End and Aim" appeared in the 2016 edition of NOON.

The Editors proudly congratulate Souvankham Thammavongsa, whose stories "Paris" and "Mani Pedi" were included in *The Journey Prize Stories 28: The Best of Canada's New Writers* (Penguin Random House, 2016).

The Editors proudly congratulate Clancy Martin, whose novel *Bad Sex* (Tyrant Books, 2015) was included in *The Guardian*'s list of the "Top 10 Failed Romances in Fiction" in January 2016.

THE LADY FROM CONNECTICUT

CHRISTINE SCHUTT

Nearly alone on the station platform, she is a heavy, heaving woman, encircled with luxe bags that scuff the pavement when she leans over and sighs. The reassuring blood rush to the head says she's alive with the body's store of surprises, the ticks and pricks and stars bright as foil when she opens her eyes. Shadow movement in the parking lot, nothing more, a quiet beseeming a bedroom suburb. She pokes at her phone to call home, seeing not numbers so much as the all-purpose islanded kitchen, her own, something more than a kitchen: polished granite surfaces in speckled pheasant colors. Everything put away and out of sight. Clean, clean. A built-in table and banquette—slide in, slide over, but no one is at the table or in the kitchen. Muted news flickers on the flat screen: gaudy mayhem.

The phone ceases to ring and she hears her bullshit message—the twinkly *Thanks so much for calling!*

"Hey," she says now. "It's me." She sways. "I thought you'd be here. I'm in Dart, a little tipsy." She hears herself wheeze, and they must hear, too, if they hear her at all.

Earlier tonight her friend had said, "Sweets. We're lucky. We've money in our pockets, and the night is not at all cold but clear fall and fragrant!"

Ah, who wouldn't love her friend?

"I should have married you, Bebe!" she had said, and not for the first time.

"Shoulda, coulda" was her answer—Bebe, happily divorced and in love with a younger woman.

Why wait at Dart station? Why wait in the Plexiglass shed? Why sit on a cold metal seat with holes she can feel the cold through?

Attend, and so she does and walks away from the station and toward town. She walks steadily enough, follows the yellow flares of the street trees in street light, walks on what she perceives as the upright side of the commercial street, past the jewelry store still golden despite the empty cases, past the rustic café with its washed floors and upended stools, past the gift store and the dry cleaner's scrolled script—*Trafalger's*—white walls, white counter dramatically backdropped by a heavy black curtain behind which hang bagged clothes. The ceiling light is a chandelier. Who said Dart was dangerous?

Between buildings in the back: a parking lot, plank fence,

hedge, sometimes a dumpster, but the lots look swept. Commerce ceases, the sidewalk narrows, and leaf-fall, stomped to leaf-meal, dusts her shoes.

An old sidewalk buckled and cracked in places; houses set back behind leathery rhododendrons—sullen and thuggish. She hates rhododendrons.

Big-deal ugly cerise blossoms, they belong in the forest not ringed around a house.

Her hands are hot and hurt; the handles of the luxe bags cut into them.

Carry on!

She is fifty-six but strong, and ahead at the turn is Saint Francis Church, the turn she takes when she drives to the station, but car conflicts meant the party planner for Big T's upcoming birthday drove her to the station this morning. She has not employed this planner before but has wandered through his parties, admiring his use of bent forks and burlap amid flats of fragile, fringy plants.

But the flowers are the least of preparing for Big T's party. The guests, the seating. Where to put Big T's noisy nephew, a pontificating vegetarian who makes everyone uncomfortable about food?

Set down your burden, Saint Francis says, and so she does: she sets aside her luxe bags and rubs her sore hands. She sits on a bench in front of the church, satchel in lap, there to contemplate the tonsured saint, arms beseeching, palms upturned. But such shallow—shallow hands! What could he hold out to anyone or what could anyone take hold of? Saint Francis of Assisi should have birds about his person, shouldn't he? A rabbit somewhere, a squirrel, a fox?

She misses having a dog, sweet Lucy, misses her son— misses his younger self who liked to walk with her, which is to say, enjoyed her company. Her company, what is it to be in her company?

Once Bebe fell asleep while she was talking to her. Bebe shut her eyes just as she was telling her how eclipsed she felt by everyone. *Am I so dull, so repetitious, so petty?* she was asking this when Bebe's eyes, she saw, were shut!

"You're angry," Bebe said tonight and has said before, along with *You can be mean*; *You can be judgmental.* Early in the evening Bebe had told her, *Stop! Stop complaining!* She had arrived angry and shopped-out and sure she had bought the wrong tie and a shirt her husband would never wear but that was because he was so . . . *Stop! You wonder why friends don't want to see you?*

Oh, lady from the suburbs, after too much wine in the city, don't cry!

On the phone again, she clicks off when she hears herself saying. . . *"No one is at home. . ."*

Not true! Tommy might be plugged in somewhere in the house.

And his father, Big T, most likely asleep on the couch, an open book across his chest, a fat hardback on some crisis the usual bullies brought about and then made money fixing.

Big T has very large hands. His hands are so big he could pulverize the plaster statue of Saint Francis with one of them. She puts her head through the harness of her satchel and moves to take up the luxe bags, but puts them aside again and sits back on the bench.

When Big T was a boy—nine or ten?—he threw potatoes at his mother. While his older brother cheered him on, he pelted her in the back.

Why didn't you stop me, Mother?

Oh, you were only trying to make your brother laugh.

Jokes at the expense of someone else can make Big T laugh, too.

In the picture of this scene her mother-in-law stands stoutly at the sink dressed in rough linen. The woman's hair is still brown and matches the brown of the sack she wears as a dress. She might be a potato!

Oh, the statue of Saint Francis is pitiably featureless, and she scolds herself for self-pity. Stand up! Quit blubbering! Raise your arms! You're alive! You're well. Think of the war-ravaged poor rocking in a boat in the middle of a black sea, desperate: you're not one of those.

How dark and separate is the house next to the church behind its spiky hedge of arborvitae—who lives there?

She has not always lived in Connecticut.

Once, she knew the lucky girl's life in Maryland. The fields and fences, mown meadow, stubble and stalk—she would like to be back on the footpath to the house on the hill in a rural-route setting, a gentleman's farm with a barn and horses cared for by loving staff. Jessup—she misses him. Once gardens simply happened and she, slender, was photographed in them.

House light through the trees but steadily darker along what turns into the stony ledge of road beside genuinely old stone walls where once she used to walk with Lucy, sweet dog.

Why haven't they turned the ledge into a broader path for dog owners—or runners, for that matter, walkers? There are no walkers that's why—or very few. She might right this imbalance. She might take up walking to the station on the days, like today, when she works in the city.

She steps into the ditch before a car passes, but its lights catch parts of her.

She is impossible to miss with these impressive bags and the color of her coat. But her bags! She put them down. She put them down on the bench at Saint Francis Church and never took them up again but walked past when she left the churchyard. She must not have cared—she doesn't care. Expensive clothes for Big T's big birthday. Sixty.

Is this gift to be returned, I wonder? Is this one for UPS? Big T is well-known to ask of all her gifts as he unwraps them—actually asks of gifts given him by anyone. Big T does not reserve his scorn for her alone.

One for the truck, back on the truck, a doozy for the truck, I'm afraid: *load her up, a return, yes, sir, a return* all Big T terms pelted like potatoes, meant to be funny, wasn't, was never, oh . . . don't get lost in neverland.

Once upon a time Big T was *Tom* to her and never wrong.

Once upon a time . . . she bought him a green cashmere sweater (he looks good in green) but this green didn't work, and he returned the sweater and came home horrified at how much she had spent on him—but also seeming happy about it. A few weeks later he bought the same sweater on sale in wheat.

She prays her bags fall into needy hands. Do your best, Saint Francis. Besides talking to animals, what else did Saint Francis do? Why is he a saint in the first place? What part of us can he protect?

What a shitty spiritual education she has had; she's simply brushed past churches all of her life, knows a crèche when she sees one.

Across the road and ahead, the pillowy landscape of the golf course and the secular life in light: the River Club badged in deep blue, gold, and white. She owns a lot of RC highball glasses because the River Club is a *big* part of Big T's life. She can turn anything into a joke with *big* at the front.

At this hour the road is not much traveled; its residents, living far apart and withdrawn into their woods and behind their fences, are abed.

Cars pass, several in a row, from a party, perhaps, following each other home—sober drivers, she hopes, soberer than she, yet she moves back into the ditch, which isn't a ditch so much as a broad rut filled with fallen leaves and broken branches, fieldstone and mist rising over a landscape pieced as quaintly as a quilt, and the lady from Connecticut a loose stitch in it.

BUBBLE

RHOADS STEVENS

There we saw baskets that were bigger than bathtubs full of small, shiny green peppers. In a covered area, where seafood was sold, we saw piles of crabs. They were still alive, climbing over one another, making bubbles. I got close to them to see them making bubbles, and in one of the bubbles I saw a little fucked human.

I, A LIAR

RHOADS STEVENS

It was something we decided to do after having argued for three hours. We had argued about whether or not I, a liar, had lied.

My fiancée and I took off all our clothes and didn't have swimsuits, because we had not planned to go to the pond today.

We were floating and swimming when a man drove by in a sedan slow enough to see us. "You can swim there?" he shouted at us. His sedan was shiny, and he stopped it.

He got out of his car, opened one of its rear doors, and a large dog came out. The dog was as big as a foal and had hair as short and dark as a panther's. As it got closer, I saw it was missing an ear. Much of its face looked burned. The man climbed down where we had climbed down, and the dog did, too.

"He loves me," the man said about the dog. "I saved him. We loved each other in a past life."

He took off his clothes, and, like us, he must not have had a swimsuit, because he got into the pond naked.

"Come on in," the man said to the dog, but the dog would not get into the water. The dog sat on a rock. "Come on in," the man said. "He watches TV with me. I got him a chair."

The man swam toward us. The dog seemed to have grown even bigger, sitting on that rock. In its burn, there was swirling purple, gray, and pink.

"I got that car because the dog liked it," the man said. "I went to the dealer, and I told the dealer, 'If you can get that dog to get in one of these cars, then, right now, I'll buy one.' That dog is the love of my life."

But the dog would not get into the water, no matter how much the man called.

"She loves me!" I said to the man. "She obeys me." Pointing at my fiancée, I said, "And I got her a chair!"

ONE DAY

MIKA YAMAMOTO

He put his cup in the sink, and—because he was still Ben, still a good husband—he leaned over and kissed me, his wife, albeit drily. Still wife, still a good wife, I stretched up to meet him.

"Please," he said, good husband that he was, "please stay safe until I get back."

I nodded because I could not speak.

With that, Ben collected my boys—his boys—our boys.

As they walked out the door, I heard Rei say, "But I don't get it."

When they were all gone, I sat down, alone. I wanted to have a cup of coffee to hold, but the act of pouring the coffee was too mundane to bear. How could I pull a cup out of the cupboard—as I always did—take the milk out of the refrigerator and pour a splash in the cup—as I always did—take the converted-from-a-honeypot sugar bowl down and spoon out sugar into my cup—as I always did—put my hand on the coffeepot, pull out the coffeepot, pour the coffee from the coffeepot—

How could I do this, all this, so normal, on a day when nothing was normal? Rei, not on the bus, but getting to school by Dad. Leo, too, getting to day care by Dad. Ben, not going to work, taking both boys to school and day care. Rei going to school with no lunch. Green Jell-O, still jiggling on counter, on plate, instead of packed in lunch. Blackened octopi in boxes. Cucumbers—not cut up into hearts for lunch. How could I possibly pour coffee in my kitchen on a day like this? I couldn't, I couldn't. So I sat, without coffee, at the table, my elbows on the table, my hands in prayer, my lips on my hands. Only, I did not pray.

CHICKEN

BRANDON HOBSON

Back when I was doing cocaine, we found a chicken in our yard. We weren't sure how it got there, but it wouldn't leave. My wife made me take a broom outside to try to scare it away.

"It's just a chicken," I said.

"You're a chicken," she said.

I didn't want to scare it, but I took the broom outside anyway. The chicken stepped away from me as I approached. The chicken looked at me, vigilant, sidelong.

"Be a good chicken," I said.

I was wearing my pajama pants and slippers. A car drove by slowly and I tried not to look odd.

I went back inside and found my wife who said, "You didn't scare it away?"

"That chicken is here for a reason," I told her.

My wife said, "What's wrong with you? Are you drunk or something?"

"The chicken will lay eggs," I said. "This is good. It's a sign or good omen. We shouldn't scare the chicken, we should keep it."

"Are you afraid of that chicken?" she said. "Is that what you're afraid of? What are you afraid of?"

I turned and hurried upstairs to the bathroom and locked the door. I did a line of cocaine and looked at myself in the mirror. My face was pale and weary. The sunlight on my face looked like shards of glass. I sat on the floor with my back against the wall and waited for my wife to come and to overawe me.

THE DAMN FOOL

BRANDON HOBSON

At home, they kept the boy in a chicken coop, and he slept there all night like a dirty chicken, coming out to eat and play.

When he jumped on the old mattress in the backyard, they put him in the chicken coop.

When he threw a stick at the neighbor's dog, they put him in the chicken coop.

Anytime—they put him in the chicken coop when he pissed himself, when he chewed with his mouth open.

His grandparents were old, and his grandfather was going blind from diabetes, so there were more-important problems to deal with.

At school, on the playground, he sometimes pretended to be a dog and barked at the other kids.

A photographer came and took photos of him at school.

"We have a serious problem," the school principal said to the grandmother. The principal was a dumpy man with ugly moles on the side of his face.

"The problem concerns hygiene," the principal said.

The grandmother, sitting across from him, was wearing dark glasses.

"It's about the chicken coop," the principal continued. "It's about personal hygiene and the chicken coop."

The grandmother sat forward, holding her cane. "Yap, that's what you do. Yap, yap, yap. Yap. Yap. Yap."

The principal didn't respond.

The boy was on the floor, covering his ears. Like a higher animal, he was whispering to himself.

I ALWAYS THOUGHT OF HER AS SO TIRED

LUCIE ELVEN

I always thought of her as so tired because she sighed and didn't make an effort to liven me up at those parties, and I was well-known, and lots of people wanted to liven me up. So it seemed like she was mistaken, that that was a mistake on her part, that she should give herself a little push. She seemed to know she could intensify and tried to avoid it. A look from her could flush my mind. But there we are. Months later, in a similar scenario, she spoke bitterly about a friend of mine, the great Nelson Spinoza, who had given her up, and that was my cue to leave. At what cost? No more flushing. No knowing if she was tired, as I now suspect, simply because she did more than us. She seemed embarrassed that she had to think about what she wanted for herself, like it was hard for her to participate in her best interests.

I could have helped her get a position nearer to home. We can all agree that she had been traveling too far to get to work.

She was a mess, she had told me. "When I'm on the motorway, when the houses I pass with their windows lit in the dark look like low carriages of trains riding alongside, I come back to the quality of reason in his driving—even when it's a late, hourslong night trip to the country and back—reversing back, that is, into my garage in the city. Where will he park his car without me? He'll be forced to take the megacoach, with a bottle of water."

I could tell it was confusing. He was a nasty little hatemaker, Nelly Spinoza.

One day it was summery and the air had come in warm shelves. She said the coffee tasted like wet suits, and the tea fishy.

When I'd seen her again, she was in a daze deciding whether what he had done to her was something she might have chosen to do of her own volition or something she would never have thought of doing—why not? She didn't ask the right questions about what she really wanted, because it was under her nose, or she didn't seize the day, or what? No.

She didn't give herself a push, a kick. Of course, why should she want to go and be a nasty little hatemaker?

PAINTINGS

JANA PALECKOVA

R. Fischer   Graslitz.

22.

23.

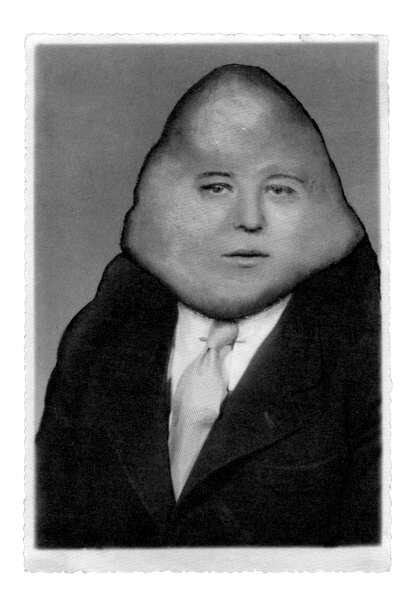

27.

30.

31.

S. Frey

WIEN XII.
Schönbrunnerstr. 275.

32.

Jos. Homolka

KLADNO

34·

 J.F. LANGHANS A SPOL.
C.A.K. DVORNÍ FOTOGRAFOVÉ.

35.

36.

38.

All paintings are untitled,
except for the painting on page 32, which is entitled *Otik*.
Date: 2015
Medium: Oil on found photograph
Dimensions: Variable

(Images have been provided courtesy of the artist
and the Fred Giampietro Gallery, New Haven, Connecticut.)

LAST LOOSENING:
A HANDBOOK FOR IMPOSTERS
AND THOSE WHO ASPIRE TO BE

Excerpts translated from the German by Lydia Davis

WALTER SERNER

TRAINING

342. Avoid people who live in such an unpleasantly moist atmosphere that you experience a thirst for fresh water. And in fact drink a glass as soon as you leave them. Then you won't think about them anymore.

344. If suddenly you no longer have the energy to lie, then at least be cruel.

346. Wait as long as you can before making use of the means that will achieve your objective as quickly as possible. Every speedy action requires a great expenditure of energy.

347. If you are not beautiful, it is generally twice as hard for you. But very often you could spare yourself half the effort if

you put a beautiful person next to you and, if necessary, leave him behind in your place.

352. Don't dance too much. Only as long as you enjoy it or for special reasons.

353. Always nurture several projects. One day you will suddenly complete one which, almost without your knowing it, has ripened inside you.

354. Your head works even without its wanting to. This you notice most clearly if you have ever spent four weeks in a small, boring health resort. Suddenly you are simply bursting with plans and ideas.

357. If you should fall ill, go into hiding. That way you will get well faster.

358. Hold out your hand to each person in such a way that no special emphasis is noticeable. And as seldom as possible.

359. Also greet people with your eyes or a smile. Never by opening your mouth.

360. Never lean back in your chair while you're speaking. It interferes with your thinking and pronunciation.

362. Restrict all exertions to a minimum. They make one old.

363. As you approach forty, start becoming especially generous. This will keep you fresh longer.

364. You must not have a family. (How you behave toward your parents and siblings is unimportant, since you do not make a show of them. Everything in South America or dead.)

365. Do not live with anyone. It enervates you without your being aware of it.

444. Regard every ear that is within earshot as a hostile one. Woe betide you if you say to yourself: "Oh, he's only an old man."

446. Always assume the walls have ears.

447. Never entirely trust a lawyer. They have so much to do with the authorities.

452. In your hotel room do important things only very quietly and next to a curtained window.

459. If you quite often see men in dark glasses, you shouldn't be surprised if you're staying in Nice. In Vienna it would have to make you suspicious.

466. Don't visit anyone at dusk.

472. Even when you think you're absolutely safe, make a decisive move as though you were being pursued.

476. Don't stand around on street corners. People might think you are looking for something there. Don't stop in the front entrances of houses. People might think you're mixed up in some strange trouble or a foolish love affair. But go as often as possible to the train station. People will think you're coming from a trip or that you're killing time before going off on one.

478. Often stand in front of mirrors in shops. This way you can comfortably observe what is going on behind you.

CLOTHING AND MANNERS

514. Everyone must have the impression that you don't know you have a cigarette between your fingers.

517. When you're eating, show that you have an appetite, but neither hurry nor be excessively slow. The more expertly and elegantly you eat, the more often you'll be invited.

518. When you eat, always employ some little techniques that are new and advantageous to execute. This can make you popular more quickly than a two-hour conversation.

519. Under no circumstances should you ever give off a smell of laundry (bleach) or soap.

520. Don't ever wear silk shirts. Unless you want to be a cattle trader or a department manager.

521. The way you move your hat in greeting should always be the same. Only allow your face and eyes to be different.

524. Never look up at the sky or down at the earth.

WARNINGS

531. In every city there are hotels whose staff collaborate with career criminals. (Before you go to sleep, put a chair against the door and set a pitcher of water on the edge of it.)

MONEY AND LETTERS

560. An effective way of achieving your goal is to fire off a dozen letters one after another.

563. If you don't want to answer an important but to you very unpleasant letter, let the sender know through a third person that you have suffered a hemorrhage and gone off to a sanatorium.

565. Love letters are *the* height of folly.

566. Be neither generous nor stingy. And only in very special cases be profligate.

567. Don't give too large a tip to the bartender at an elegant nightclub. Otherwise he will size you up for what you are.

570. Don't love money too much, so that, when the situation requires it, you can without difficulty decide to undertake nothing for weeks at a time. Some have even died prematurely because they couldn't resist the habit of spending a few thousand every month.

571. Risk only money. Never your freedom. Better to wash dishes. It will do less harm to your élan than four days in prison.

573. If you get to know a financier, immediately propose a transaction to him, however fanciful it may be. He will doubtless show no interest in it, but he will remember you. And one day perhaps propose one to you.

MRS. LYMAN

ROB WALSH

This is a terribly traditional beginning and so slow I've probably already lost some of you, but Mrs. Lyman was a traditional woman. By that I mean she dressed conservatively and she never swore or refused to back her husband's outlook. Even if he obviously had his sights on my mother.

I won't traffic in any gossip about Mr. Lyman and my mother, I should establish that up front—this is about Mrs. Lyman.

I was only a child when I first met her and seldom got a good look at her. Every once in a while the light in that particular room would tilt, at least that was how it felt when new lengths of sun would make it through the curtains and, well, maybe I should stop here. The bare minimum of what you need to know about Mrs. Lyman's skin is that this was before moisturizers were any good. Back then it was all chemical-filled gel designed to dry you out even further and necessitate the application of more and more. My mother kept a huge tub of this on her dresser and was always monitoring its level and running off to the store when it got too low. I expect that Mrs. Lyman was no different.

The point I'd like to make is that Mrs. Lyman kept to the shadows allocated by her husband or my mother, but they are both dead now.

She had very little money left. What had happened to it all? That was a mystery. Her husband was a successful architect, mainly churches, and had a standard life-insurance policy that should have been enough to keep Mrs. Lyman going.

I probably should have begun here, with the job I offered Mrs. Lyman. She had always been so nice to me. Her cookies were extremely sweet, but nobody knew about refined sugars back then and I am not diabetic or anything, so no real harm came of it.

No, if I really knew what I was doing I would have started the story with the blackmail, with the money Mrs. Lyman extorted from me, but it's so hard to begin there. She wasn't an evil woman, not even a bad woman. She *looked* evil because of that terrible moisturizer that she *still* used even though I religiously gifted her little bottles of shea butter and coconut oil. But let's get back to the job I offered her.

What I thought was that she could come over a few times a week—she could choose the days and times—and tidy my place a bit. I didn't even need anyone to tidy up. The house was fine and I was proud of its condition. But this way Mrs. Lyman could still afford to feed herself and pay for cable.

I never considered her a housekeeper or servant, but I permitted her to choose what to call the position if she wanted to call it anything at all. "We don't even have to put a name on it," I said.

"No, I suppose we don't," Mrs. Lyman said in her quiet voice. Her husband was very loud, boisterous, and this quiet voice folded perfectly beneath his. "No, it can be dangerous to put a name to things. Best to keep one's names hidden."

What was she talking about? Don't worry about that; Mrs. Lyman was pretty old and spent a lot of time by herself.

Like I said, you'll have to forgive her this commentary. It ended soon enough and she agreed to the terms of the job. Mrs. Lyman was paid a dollar an hour above what other housekeepers and servants in the neighborhood were getting paid. She was terrible at her job, admittedly, and sometimes the house seemed dirtier for her efforts. I found little piles of ash in the basement corner where she smoked without thinking I would find out about it. But I wanted to help her financially without making her seem like a charity case. Also, I thought, it would give her a sense of accomplishment, the sense that she was alive in a world that understood she was alive.

This continued for about a year. Her condition improved considerably. I'll guess she gained twenty, twenty-five pounds. The bags under her eyes remained, but her face seemed to have doubled in color. "You look fantastic, Mrs. Lyman," I told her, "and because you're doing so well it might be time for me to bring up the cigarette ashes in the basement."

"I don't know what you're talking about."

"Well, this is not easy for me to say, because I was only a little child when you were in your prime, but Mrs. Lyman, I must insist that you stop smoking down there."

"What if I refuse to admit I have any idea what you're talking about?"

"Well, I won't terminate you. I would never terminate you."

"I see," she said. "But you have introduced, at least, the concept of termination."

"No," I said.

"I never smoke down there. It is somebody else," she said.

"Who, Mrs. Lyman?"

"I cannot say the name. In many ways you remain a child, a lamb, and I will not scourge your home with its name."

"Understood," I said finally.

"I'm going to change the subject now, for your own protection," she said. "But since you're bringing up those ashes in the basement, I'm going to bring up your mother—and my husband."

"Mrs. Lyman, what do you mean?"

"Everybody in town knows what I mean."

I nodded grimly. "About the affair."

"The most public and splashy affair there ever was," she said, "and—well, would you like me to continue?"

"No."

"Then I have ended this conversation?"

I paid her in cash and walked her to the door. This was the first time I started to see her as a threat. She was getting stronger with the regular money I provided. What was also getting stronger was the cigarette smell in the basement. I couldn't go down there anymore. The ashes, I had noticed last time I went down there, were piled in an oddly vertical manner.

When I terminated her, Mrs. Lyman smiled—kind of—and produced a cell phone that had gone missing months ago.

"Does this look familiar to you?" she asked.

I reached out to claim the phone but she put it back into her purse. "And do you happen to recall what's on this phone?"

"Private material."

"Private material, yes. Let's call it that. You said my job was to cleanse this home of filth, so of course I needed to remove this material."

"Mrs. Lyman," I said calmly, "everyone these days has naked pictures on their phone—"

She held up her hand. "Something I have learned in the last few years," she said, "is that I like having regular income again. This will continue indefinitely. If it ever stops, I will release these pictures to everyone you know."

In my opinion, those pictures were artistic and beautiful. There was even something kind of thrilling about others seeing them. Since I would not be publishing the pictures myself, nobody could accuse me of vanity or exhibitionism. Instead, I thought, the broad release of those pictures would garner tremendous sympathy. People could see and admire the body I worked hard for at the gym, the results of yoga and a natural diet, and at the same time I would rid myself of Mrs. Lyman's wages and her piles of cigarette ash. Things could not have turned out better for me, if I looked at it like that.

But I was still thinking about the affair my mother had had with Mrs. Lyman's husband. "Oh, no, Mrs. Lyman," I said, "please don't release those pictures."

"What I *should* release is the author of those ashes in your basement," she said cryptically, "and try to tether that author permanently to this home. Smell my breath," she said, getting up to blow in my face. "Do you smell cigarettes?"

"No, Mrs. Lyman."

"Exactly. Well, listen—you keep paying my wages. And I'll keep coming here to clean."

"That won't be necessary," I said. "I'll pay you, but you no longer have to come here."

"I like coming here."

"Yes, but—"

"I shall continue to come here, or—" She raised the phone threateningly. "Now walk me to the door."

Once, I set down a plate of cookies that were not store-bought but homemade, sweetened only with agave nectar. They also contained carob chips and goji berries and, in my opinion, were irresistibly healthy and satisfying. When Mrs. Lyman did not touch the cookies, I placed the tray next to her ash sculptures in the basement.

There were always cookies at her Sunday meetings with my mother, not that this deserves more than ordinary consideration, but it's a memory from a long time ago and for whatever reason these cookies remain the brightest part.

Both women avoided church on Sundays and were quite vehement about keeping clear of other holy sites, but as a child you do not think too much about this, you just eat your cookies.

Mrs. Lyman remained in my employ for the next ten years. One day, however, Mrs. Lyman did not ascend from the basement and I assumed correctly that she had died down there.

I'M COMING FOR YOUR CHILD

ROB WALSH

I'm Coming for Your Child was probably the scariest movie we had ever seen, and the movie entered conversations with our friends or coworkers usually when someone asked what was wrong, and we kind of acted surprised and said nothing, nothing was wrong, and they said obviously something is bothering you—that was all it took to get us talking.

Once, my wife woke up in the night and her hand flopped around looking for the light switch. This was a week after we saw the film. Maybe I should mention she always slept through the night, flattened into a pale, aging mass that was getting harder to cuddle, but like a good husband I only said supportive things and even claimed she was still sexy in her nightgown, even beautiful. We're divorced now, is why I'm telling you this.

But we loved each other quite a bit at the time and said whatever was necessary to comfort the person and help them feel better about themselves. I held her until she stopped crying. Not crying as in tears, but staring at the ceiling and ranting incoherently. Well, incoherently if you've never seen *I'm Coming for Your Child*. If you've seen the film, you know exactly what she was going through and could probably even decipher her words, those being the same words of the mother in the scene near the end, the scene where they look everywhere in the bedroom for a potential intruder but forget to check the ceiling above them.

We forgot the movie after a few months. A few years later, we could even begin to laugh at it—isn't that what usually happens? I mean, some parts you can never laugh at. I'm talking about what happens to the family pets. We cannot partially condone or even crack a smile at anything happening to pets. We're animal people. Now that I think this through, we never laughed at any aspect of *I'm Coming for Your Child*, it was too fucked-up, but almost every other scary movie that initially bothered us did turn into a joke over time.

All of this worked as a setup to our meeting the director. We were at a party. It wasn't Hollywood or even California, but you can think of it that way if it's more convenient. It was crowded, dark. We were all drinking a punch. What sort of punch? Full of little seeds that had been presoaked in another, stronger alcohol, maybe tequila. Well, it was having its effect on my wife. "Maybe you should let me finish that for you," I told her. To a stranger passing nearby I said kind of self-consciously, "She's not usually like this." But the stranger continued on without noticing us.

When I tried to take the cup from my wife, she twisted away. I tried again. What had gotten into her? It was best not to force the issue, since she had started going to the gym every morning and I didn't know how strong she was now. I glanced around to see if anyone had witnessed my failure to get the cup from her. It didn't seem like anyone had noticed. But getting outmaneuvered like that did not feel good. And now she was getting flirty.

We had been married for a while at this point and had an unspoken agreement that she was allowed to flirt with other guys when she got like this, but they had to be harmless ones. She was honoring that. She had chosen a medium-sized man. The room was ill-lit, but it didn't conceal his great, outstanding ears and an orb-shaped paunch below his black T-shirt. If push came to shove, I could take him down, I thought, looking hard at the man.

As you've probably figured out, this was the director of *I'm Coming for Your Child*. But he did not tell us that right away. In fact, he didn't even mention he was a director. She put a hand on his leg and asked what he did. All he said was that he worked in the film industry. It was the sort of party where everyone said that. And where is the harm in getting up close to him and speaking those cute little half words into his mouth, or playfully bumping against him every now and then?

What happened, I guess, was that the director was accustomed to women flirting with him, since *I'm Coming for Your Child* attracted a certain type of groupie. What also happened, looking back, was that our marriage was at a rough patch, and I was unreasonably concerned that others at the party had witnessed her rebuffing my attempt to take away the cup of punch. I was acting disinterested, not paying attention to her. And then, when I turned around, she was gone.

No, she hadn't been abducted, just pushed against the sink in one of the upstairs bathrooms, she later admitted, her head partway descended into the sink while the director helped himself to a fistful of her hair. He was so used to the groupies that he was in total control now, programmed to whisper memorable lines from *I'm Coming for Your Child* while he worked the groupies from behind. Remember, she admitted everything to me and later said that she wasn't really pushed against the sink but had agreed to position herself like that, but also remember that my wife didn't know he was the director until he started whispering that stuff from the movie, like, the guy who calls and tells them exactly where they are and what they're presently doing in the house even though all the curtains are drawn.

We went to a marriage counselor about it.

"Please, be seated whenever you're ready," the counselor said. "You can call me Alexandra. After you've had some time to shed that dreary waiting room and adjust to the warmth of my cozy office, I want you to look at one another, and when you are ready, tell each other what you see."

"The director of *I'm Coming for Your Child*," I said immediately, seeing his ears and his paunch. "That's one of our problems. I can't look at her without seeing the director."

"Why don't you tell her, not me," Alexandra said, "why this bothers you so."

I looked back at my wife, then back at Alexandra. "I don't want to hurt her anymore. This experience kind of messed her up. That movie really scared her. The movie's . . . inhuman. And then, without any warning, the director of that movie was inside her." I thought of how I could communicate the rest of our difficulties to Alexandra. "The experience messed both of us up," I said finally, red-faced because I had thought of like ten other ways of putting it but they all fell apart in my head.

Alexandra said to my wife, "Hello? Hello? Are you there?"

I said, "Don't snap your fingers at her, Alexandra."

The marriage counselor was writing a fair number of notes in her ledger, and she asked me, without looking up, if she could expect my wife to be a verbal participant in today's session.

"Have you ever seen *I'm Coming for Your Child*?" I asked.

She thought about it. "You're not supposed to ask me questions. However, is that the one where the little man has been living in their basement all the while?"

I nodded.

She continued writing on the pad. "Is it the one where the other, masked man keeps appearing in the same public bathrooms as the father?"

I nodded. "And scooting into the urinal right next to his, yes."

What happened after that—and I'm pretty sure this wasn't

supposed to happen—was that Alexandra put down the notepad and delivered her half-baked philosophy on horror movies. "We like such movies," Alexandra concluded, "because they remind us of comforts we have ceased to respect. We might be depressed, or our marriage might be failing, but at least we are not badly burned or lacerated. We are intact, and urged to appreciate our intactness."

My wife looked up for the first time at Alexandra and said these days she didn't feel intact.

"She speaks," Alexandra said. "You're contradicting me, but all right. I'll take what I can get. Go on. Tell me how you feel."

My wife poked me in the ribs, the signal for me to answer for her. "She thinks part of her soul has been stolen."

"And do you indulge this theory?" Alexandra asked me, smiling a smile we didn't like.

I looked out the window that gave onto the parking lot, the only window in the little office, and kept my mouth shut. Alexandra then flipped to another page and asked if we would mind reconstructing the so-called party, with special attention to what happened in the bathroom upstairs.

I got up and poured a glass of water. It had been my plan to toss the water in Alexandra's face, but I've had thousands of plans like that and they never amount to anything. We didn't like Alexandra. As my wife and our marriage started to recover, we communicated more at home. Often the topic was that bitch Alexandra. Behind the polish, she was mean and petty. She liked to abuse the power dynamic, and seemed almost greedy to hold sway over vulnerable people. As much as I hate to admit it, these were big reasons why I pursued her. I still had to get even with my wife for cheating on me with the director. More than anything else, Alexandra could help us this way.

"We really shouldn't be doing this," Alexandra would say. We visited a string of cheap motels but her line was always the same. "We shouldn't, we can't. It's a horrible breach of ethics. No more. Let's end here for today," just like she would say during her counseling sessions, and act like she was collecting her clothes off the floor. "But what about your wife?" she would say when I dragged her back to the bed. "Visualize that she is here," Alexandra would say, "watching, but you still can't stop yourself, can you, even though she's in the room with us right now— you must try to visualize that."

No, that never happened. I never did any of that with Alexandra. This is just what I thought about during our sessions. Her advice wasn't much use. It was usually trite, condescending, and designed mainly to frustrate us, and the motel scenario just grew from that. I wouldn't disrespect my wife with someone like Alexandra, not even after what happened with the director.

I need to be honest. What really happened was that we did go to those motels. I've never admitted it before. Obviously, Alexandra was not attracted to me, she was a 9 and I was like a 4.5, and that's why she kept on invoking my wife, I think, because my body wasn't exciting enough. I've never been happy with my body and she never complimented it during our motel stays, and seemed always to be looking away from it, toward the shadows where she liked to pretend my wife was hiding, watching everything.

It was almost immediately after we suspended contact with Alexandra that things started looking up for us. But this was also around the time we ran into the director again.

We loved each other, we had said so that morning, and then a few hours later my wife went for an audition.

She came back with some bad news. "He's an executive producer," she said.

I don't remember what I was eating. I do know that I kept eating it like nothing was the matter. It wasn't clear yet what she was talking about and there was no reason not to continue on as if everything were normal.

"I got the part, but he's an executive producer. I never would have tried out for the part if I'd known."

Let me say that although my wife is a gifted actress, she had never gotten a part before. She hardly ever went to auditions anymore. There was an incident, one we don't like to talk about. A casting manager who left the room in the middle of her scene. My wife finished the scene to an empty room. She waited. Hours later a secretary came in and said oh, hello, I'm sorry, you can go home now. Anyway, now she worked at the office-supply store. "Take it," I told her. "You've got to take it."

"I don't know. I never would have tried for it had I known he was affiliated."

"You have to take it!" I grabbed her by the shoulders and kind of shook her encouragingly. She argued with a special grace, but I was louder than I had ever been inside our cramped apartment. The director would, I knew, absorb her fully, even if he was not the director but the executive producer. "Take it!" What started as shoulder-grabbing had become a fierce hug, and both of us were crying. Whether I wanted her to take it or not, I'm still not sure. But I knew what I had to say.

TO KNOW IS TO KNOW THAT YOU KNOW

Excerpt from a memoir in progress

CLANCY MARTIN

For a long time I remembered that I was raped by two of my stepbrothers, and that I saw them rape other kids in our family.

It was a furnace room. It was at the bottom of the basement stairs, on the right, behind my stepfather's tool room and the refrigerator where, once a month, we stored the two cases of many different kinds of soda my mom bought at the Pop Shoppe. My older brother's favorite was black cherry, my favorite was cream soda, and I don't remember what my little brother liked. We would take one of my stepfather's nails and his hammer and very carefully tap a small hole in the tin cap of the bottle, and then shake the soda with a thumb over the top and spray it into our mouths.

I would run past the furnace room when I got near the bottom of the stairs and was going into the basement room, which was our TV room and sometimes a playroom. For a long time we had a Ping-Pong table that friends had loaned us, and then one day they came and picked it up.

At the back of my stepfather's narrow tool room with his long high workbench and the tools hanging on the wall was the furnace itself, and behind the furnace was the furnace room. It was a tight squeeze to get past the furnace into the furnace room. I had to sidle through even when I was six or seven and I was a scrawny kid. There was no light in the furnace room unless the furnace was on, aside from the little bit of light that came in from the bulb hanging in the tool room, and the other little bit of light that came in from my stepbrothers' closet. My stepbrothers had cut a hole in the wall of the closet of their bedroom so that they could squeeze into the furnace room that way.

Two of my stepbrothers lived in that basement bedroom during the time I am describing, which lasted about five years, ages six to eleven for me. Then they moved out of the house and the basement lost all of its terror and its excitement.

I was an easily frightened child—I wouldn't let my hands hang off the bed when I slept, and I didn't like to shower because you had to close your eyes—but that furnace room scared me more than anything else. I wouldn't get a soda out of the basement refrigerator unless my older brother, my little brother, or one of my stepsisters came with me.

I can very precisely see where and how they did it in the furnace room and even the looks on their faces. I hadn't planned on writing about any of this while my mother was still alive. It explained a lot, those childhood rapes: my unusually depressed childhood, my many suicide attempts, my alcoholism, and the addictions—the depression, death, suicide, and even murder that haunted our family. It made sense to me that my stepbrothers were violently angry, because my mother and stepfather married imprudently quickly after my stepsiblings' mother died. She died unexpectedly and violently from a particularly savage form of cancer, and less than year later they had a new mother and new brothers whom their new mother very obviously preferred. They couldn't attack her, so they attacked us, in ways that we were forced to keep secret. They were teenagers and we were kids.

But now I suspect I made the whole thing up over the years.

I was lying in bed late on a Sunday morning, in Kansas City where I live, waiting for my wife to text. She was in a cave in Nepal. She was with friends of ours so I wasn't too worried about her. But she had tonsillitis so there was reason to be worried. I worried about other things too: would she fall in love while she was traveling? Would she realize she didn't want to be married? Would she decide she shouldn't come back to our quiet midwestern life with its clingy humdrum details, its boredom, its muddiness, its lusterlessness? She'd lived her life before us in Houston, New York, and Seattle, and she despises Kansas City, which I understand. When friends from New York visit us here they hold their noses.

I teach at a modest city university here—it's walking distance from our house, though these days I always drive—and once a friend of mine, a New Yorker, observed to another friend and former lover of mine, another New Yorker: "If he were any good, would he be teaching there?"

But I was raised in Calgary, Alberta, a cow town, a Canadian redneck oil town, home of the Calgary Stampede, formerly the world's largest rodeo, and I am comfortable here in Kansas City. I may be anesthetized, biding my time, hiding.

My mother left my father for a man named Blair who had seven children. I was five when we all moved in together; my older brother Darren was twelve; my younger brother Pat was three. Blair and Pat took to each other and later, in the years before my father's death at the age of fifty-seven, Pat no longer acknowledged our dad and took Blair as his father. I always hated Blair, though I don't think I've ever admitted that, and I'm not sure I should write it down now, while my mother is alive.

My mother lives alone now, in Fort Worth, Texas, where she moved with Blair when my brothers and I had a jewelry business there. She and Blair first lived in an apartment building and then bought a small, pretty house two blocks from where I, my first wife and our daughter lived. My wife and I divorced not long after my mother moved to Texas to be near us and a few years after that Blair died, and now it is only my mother and her series of dogs. She's on her third since I lived in her neighborhood. At first I thought she was lonely. She missed Blair and naturally she was grieving, but she struggled with depression. I suspect that my mother and I are much more alike than I had realized, and that now, like me, she accepts the fact that we don't talk very often, that we mostly joke with each other when we talk, and that we almost never see each other. I don't think she's lonely now. Probably she would like to see me more often than she does, and I would like to be a better son in that way. But I also think she is content with our arrangement. She never calls me, and I call her once a month, maybe less, and on holidays. We text at least once a month, and she sends family news when she has it, and we have an occasional correspondence on Facebook.

My father, a self-described mystic and astral traveler, never accepted the divorce, and after a series of spiritual experiences in India, he began to write my mother long, disturbing love letters about their time together at night while she slept. The letters continued, about one a month for about ten years, almost until he died. In his letters my mother and father visited other planes of existence together, and she received instruction, from both my father and various other teachers, which was intended to help her with the ghastly karma she had created through their divorce and her subsequent remarriage. I heard these stories many times myself, driving with my father on his restless pilgrimages across the United States, but at a certain point my mother started to mail me my father's letters, and I still have them now, more than twenty years after his death.

There are many of these letters and I include an early one here. Class distinctions were a theme of the early ones. My mother came from a lower-middle-class Canadian family, my father from a wealthy one.

Again—Patrick is my younger brother, one of my two "real brothers," as opposed to stepbrothers—the youngest of all of us. Sai Baba was my father's guru and one of the most celebrated Indian spiritual leaders of the twentieth century. Blair, as I've mentioned, was my stepfather. Vickie is of course my mother. (The underlining, etc., is my father's.)

> *Dearest Vickie,*
>
> *I am sorry if this letter upsets you Darling but it must be written for karmic purposes. I know that you have no idea what Spiritual love is, because in order to know what it is, you must* <u>experience</u> *it! You have never experienced it Vic or you wouldn't be so "out to lunch" whenever we talk. You would be* <u>tuned in</u>, <u>centered</u>, *and* <u>loving</u>*!*
>
> *It's something that you will not really understand for many lives to come!*
>
> *You may ask me why I'm writing you this letter. The reason should be obvious.* <u>PATRICK</u>*! I don't know if you know what you're doing but it would seem obvious that you don't! It's very typical for a person from your level of society but I had hoped that you might have realized what you were doing and stopped it. But you haven't Darling! I talked to the "boys"* [in margin: <u>WHITE BROTHER-HOOD</u>] *last nite! They confirmed what you are doing!!!*
>
> *Vickie, I cannot find fault with you for not knowing. TO KNOW, IS TO KNOW THAT YOU KNOW. But I realize as I write this that you have no idea what I'm talking about! All I can do is pray for you and send you tapes, and books and continue my*

Astral Projection with you. The last time I came up to Calgary I <u>*think*</u> *that you were glad to see me but you are so unlike any of my other students, it's difficult to tell. Vickie, in order to receive you must become willing to* <u>*OPEN yourself completely*</u>*. Sai Baba says that you're afraid of what you may find and that's the reason! What you did in Calgary 21 years ago is going to take many, many incarnations to rectify!*

My only hope is that you realize what you have done to our children and start "a make up" process immediately!

Unconscious people never do this, "<u>*The Masses*</u>*" however are "*<u>*ASSES*</u>*" and I am sure you realize this by* <u>*NOW*</u>*!*

Please Vickie don't do anymore damage to Patrick. The boy is going to have a tough time growing up without a Father as it is!

Blair as you well know has no interpersonal skills and is really a Fool. If you don't realize this by now you soon will see it all in the Astral World.

I realize that you are extremely limited because your exposure has been so limited during the past 21 years but I ask for once that you <u>*STOP*</u> *AND* <u>*THINK*</u> *and* <u>*think*</u> *of your children and not* <u>*yourself*</u>*.*

I love you totally and I always will.

Love and light

Bill xxoxxxoxxo!

P.S. I am not responsible for anything that happens to Blair in the future. I merely reported what <u>*He*</u> *did and the manner in which he did it!*

I was at the kitchen table. We ate all of the meals that I can remember at that round heavy wooden pine-yellow kitchen table. I put a fondue fork right through my hand one night at that table, when I was nine. I still have the scar. When I was very little our cocker spaniel Sam was still alive and he lay under the table and growled. He was a sick, unhappy dog who bit. I'm sure he did not like it when we moved into the rental house with all of my stepbrothers and two stepsisters, and I expect he was teased. He was a gift from my parents to my older brother when he turned five, before I was born. There were photos of that time—during the divorce my mother had burned all but a few photos—and in the pictures they looked happy, my parents and my older brother, though I later learned that they weren't. There was even a picture of my brother when Sam was just a puppy, evidently taken on his birthday or shortly thereafter. Sam looked happy then, too, of course—he was a happy, healthy English cocker spaniel puppy in the arms of a five-year-old boy. I often looked at that picture and thought, Hmm, he was a better kid than I was and so he had a better life. This is a normal way to think: that other people's much more desirable lives are the result of their moral and personal superiority to you. And, of course, in an old color photo, if the people in the photo look happy, then the whole world they lived in looks much better than your own.

When I got home from school I would sit at the kitchen table to do my homework and talk to my mother while she made dinner. There were ten of us living in that three-bedroom house (one of my stepbrothers moved to Vancouver immediately after the marriage and another ran away from home—he later killed himself) and six ate at the table: the older kids were allowed to make a plate and leave. But in the afternoon after school that kitchen table was mine. My privacy.

"I don't have any friends. I'm not popular."

I had decided to tell my mother what was bothering me.

"Of course you're popular. You have lots of friends."

I did not have lots of friends—I had two friends, Chris P. and Tom D., and I didn't really want either of them. They were off-brand, bottom-of-the-shelf friends. Tom came from a rich family—we never went to his house, because his mother didn't like him to have friends over—and he should have been a good friend to have, but he was a bit short and a bit of a bully, so he wasn't popular. Chris was one of those shy, slightly chubby, not very smart kids who get picked on. I was in the middle of this undesirable pair, as I've almost always been in the middle of a threesome of friends. I'm a middle child—between two brothers—so I create these comfortable situations. A higher status, me, a lower status. (It occurs to me now, as a married man, with just my wife and me in the house, that this is why we have a dog.)

"Mom, I'm trying to tell you something important."

She insisted on the lie that I was one of the popular kids, and I let it go.

Later I remember, in third or fourth grade, one of the genuinely popular kids moved into a house across the street from ours because his house in a better neighborhood had caught fire and was being repaired. It was wintertime and I could see there was a group of seven or eight popular kids, from both my elementary school and another school, throwing snowballs at each other in his yard and running across the street into our yard. It was dark with the falling snow making bright white towers in the street-lights, and I kneeled on our living room sofa and watched them playing through the window.

My mom caught me. "Go out there. Those are friends of yours. Go play with them in the snow."

"Mom, I can't just go out there. They're not playing. They're having a snowball fight."

"Of course you can. That's Susan Dabbs." (I had a crush on Susan Dabbs.) "Those are all friends of yours. Go on. I'll get your coat. Put on your boots."

I knew it was a bad idea, but I also thought, Maybe this is my moment. I often had those kinds of Charlie Brown daydreams, of being picked first for soccer, of hitting a home run in softball, of beating up Sean D. during recess (a handsome Dutch bully who tyrannized me and Chris, but left Tom alone). My mother once observed that Sean was an unusually good-looking kid, which I made the mistake of repeating to Sean—I still have a tendency to flatter bullies. I have always been a coward—and for about a year after this, all through fifth grade, Sean liked to tell people, "Clancy's mom wants to fuck me." Sean was not among the group of popular kids throwing snowballs and ducking for cover behind trees up and down the street.

"They're in our front yard, Clancy. They wouldn't be playing there if they didn't want you to join them. I'm sure they can see you through the window."

I understood that I was waiting for an invitation. But I didn't know how to get invited. So I went into my own front yard and started throwing snowballs. They were confused at first and I saw some glances exchanged but then it was okay. Afterward we were going across the street to the other kid's house because his mom had made us all hot chocolate, and at the door I heard him say to another one of my friends, "I don't know how he found out. I guess he lives there. I didn't say anything." I decided to leave, and Susan Dabbs stopped me. She said: "Come in. Where are you going? We're not going home yet. None of us are going home yet."

But I already had my Moon Boots on and I was going back home. I was a sulky, angry kid and was quick to get my feelings hurt. But for months after that I wondered if my life would have changed very much for the better if I had not heard that comment or had ignored it and gone in with the rest of them to have hot chocolate and let them see that I could fit in very easily, given the chance.

Here's another of my father's letters to my mother, mostly concerning one of their astral journeys, written sometime in 1995, about seventeen years after the previous letter (the letters are not dated, but there are often internal cues for approximating their dates). Butch (whom he refers to) was a teenage friend of my parents who died young.

Darling,

I'm really thrilled that you were so thrilled last night. It's been almost 6 long years but at least now you can see what you've done and what you're going to have to make up for! It's not an easy path you've picked Vickie, but at least it will be <u>fruitful</u>.

You must remember not to be judgmental and to carry out the Brothers' orders, without question. They will NEVER ask you to do anything <u>WRONG</u>!

You had an enormous number of questions last night and I'll do my best to answer them all, in time.

Yes Darling we are together again in our next incarnation in India. Blair is there also but because of the tremendous damage done to our children this time, there will not be any direct lineage. So don't worry. Just concentrate on cleaning up the CAUSATIVE KARMA with me otherwise it could hang on for many centuries, 11 at least. As you are now approaching 55 a lot of affirmative prayer will help and I will also take you to LOGOS later in the month where you can meet Butch who is the head of the PRAYER BLOCK there. You'll enjoy seeing him again, I'm sure!

Remember when you make the decision about Blair, let me know by coming to Palm Beach astrally, it would lift 11 lifetimes of very bad KARMA for you. You've finally made a right decision after 22 years! I congratulate you! It will carry forward to your Indian birth!

I love you Darling, I've never stopped! I am only sorry that I had to complete the KARMIC WORKOUT this way because I know how difficult it's been for you and the children.

See you very soon,

Love and light,

Bill xxoxoxo

P.S. Forget the guilt! Live the <u>NOW</u>!

My mother was my best friend for the first half of my life. When I was in graduate school my first wife used to complain about the cost of our long-distance phone calls, because of the almost-nightly hour-long conversations I would have with my mother. My stepfather Blair went to therapy because of the jealousy issues our closeness created for him.

When I was suffering a crisis in the early years of my first marriage, naturally I called my mother.

"Mom, I don't think we're going to make it," I told her.

My daughter was one and a half years old at this time. She, my wife, and my brother Patrick were outside in the enormous pool at his expensive Fort Worth apartment complex—this was when my two brothers and I were in the jewelry business together—and I had lied and said that I needed to go to the bathroom because I needed to call my mom where no one could hear me. This was less than a month before I finally broke down and asked my wife for a divorce. I was still faithful to my wife at that time—the cheating started a couple of months later.

"I don't know what to do. She's depressed all the time. I'm miserable. I don't think I can do this."

My mother was quiet for a few seconds.

"I think you two should have another baby," she said.

"Mom," I said, "that's like I'm calling you to complain that I can't pay my Visa bill and you're telling me to put it on my American Express."

With my father it was different. He made it clear that there was nothing I couldn't discuss with him. When I was twelve he asked me if I'd started masturbating yet. "There's nothing to be ashamed of if you haven't, son. I just want you to know that it's natural when you do." (I had, of course, but wasn't telling him.) Later, he asked about my wife: "Are you two climaxing together yet? It can take years of practice. But it's important that you take her sexual needs as seriously as your own, son." He told me all of the intimate details of his and my mother's relationship, including details of their sex life. But of course his outrageous candor was humiliating for me—"Let's get you to a dermatologist, son." "I don't want to go to a dermatologist, Dad." "Those pimples aren't your fault, but we have to do something about them." And so I never told him anything. On reflection, I couldn't speak to either of my parents, because my mother only wanted to see the good in my life, and my father, though he didn't mean to, was always implicitly criticizing. In that way they were traditional parents like most people have, I expect.

So I never spoke with either of my parents about the rapes, how I believed I had been raped and raped over the course of years. I thought that my father suspected something when he'd make dark, elliptical comments about Blair's children and the damage they were doing to me and my younger brother. He frequently accused Blair of being gay and also of sexual deviance and I have added these suggestions to my narrative: probably Blair had raped his own kids, that's how these things happened. We were the youngest and weakest, shit rolls downhill, etc. Naturally he'd never touch us, me and my little brother, because, as my mother often told me, she'd married Blair "on condition that you never discipline my children." He was a violent man with his own kids, which I had witnessed in person many times. He couldn't get away with it. Worse still, one of my stepsisters later accused the older boys in the family of raping her repeatedly, back in those same bad days of our early crowded years of living on top of each other in that house.

But one night in Lawrence, Kansas, in 2005, after too much wine, I decided to confront my mother about it. As often when I was drunk around my mother, I was in the middle of a long maudlin harangue about the difficulties of my childhood. My second wife sat quietly, nervously beside me on the couch. She was drinking too or she would have put a stop to it.

"Everyone has a tough childhood, Clancy. When I was a girl my father got drunk and gave away my new puppy to one of the kids in our apartment building. Get over it."

"Mom, you doan know what it was like. You doan know what is like to be afraid of the basement. You knew what happened down there, didn't you? You must have known."

"I don't have any idea what you're talking about, Clancy. You've had enough wine. Don't give him any more wine. You're slurring your words."

"Mom, you know what they did to us down there. In that

furnace room. Or maybe you didn't know. They raped us down there, Mom. They made us watch."

"You're drunk. You're making this up. Go to bed. I'm going to bed."

"Mom, you know . . . " She went up the stairs and closed the door to her room.

"You're too hard on your mother," my wife said. "She has to deal with this stuff the best way she knows how. Imagine how hard that was for her. Imagine how hard it is for her now, blaming herself."

I had told my wife vivid stories about being raped by my stepbrothers, about being held down and forced to watch them rape other kids in our family, stories I believed to be true, but that even then I was beginning to doubt. I told her these stories in the hope that they would make her love me more.

Here's a third letter from my father. This letter addresses a story that I'd heard from both of my parents about their wedding night. My mother told it to me first, when I was twenty, when she told me about his affairs. Until then she had kept those secret from me.

"It started on our wedding night. Or probably before. For all I know he was cheating on me with my friends. That's what some of them said. Anyway, he got drunk, and we had an argument. So he stormed out of the hotel room. And when he came back, hours later, he woke me up and threw a pair of women's panties at me."

When I confronted my father about it, he said, "Well, she's exaggerating, son. Your mother has a slippery relationship with the truth. But yes, we had problems in the sack. We did have a big argument about it on our wedding night, that much is true. Sometimes one person's sex drive doesn't match the other's, son, and that can create real problems in a marriage."

This letter is one of the last letters my father sent my mother, before he became homeless and then died in a hospital for indigents in Miami, Florida, on the floor for mental patients.

> *Dearest darling Vickie,*
>
> *Congratulations for your work the other night! It took a great deal of effort and real "guts" to do what you did. We must be honest with ourselves first before we can be honest with others and it now looks like you are going to be able to do this at long last. As* [Sai] *Baba explained to you, life in the physical is merely an illusion and we are merely acting out parts as our KARMA dictates. Once you understand this Vickie your life will make a lot more sense.*
>
> *It's really very simple. It's really too bad that people in AA can't understand this and there would be a lot less damage done to the "NEWCOMERS."*
>
> *One other thing I should mention at this time is why I played around when we were married. My adultery Vickie was a direct payback for the adultery that you committed in 8 previous relationships. Nothing more — nothing less. That is why I felt so guilty about it and almost wanted to die because of it. From our wedding night you turned almost FRIGID. Surely you remember what an absolute disaster our wedding night was!! Well Darling you can work on this next week when we go up again.*

Don't feel guilty, you simply didn't KNOW. Fifteen years ago, when I first started studying the Mysteries in earnest, I made some real errors in judgment too! You are not alone!

You have a great deal of work to do and I'll make sure THE BROTHERS don't rush you!

I <u>love</u> you so very, very much and will make sure that you understand everything at a very <u>slow</u> pace.

Don't be afraid darling as FEAR is constructed by man and it's not real. It's only part of the illusion of the physical plane reality, that's <u>unreal</u>.

I love you Dear One and I'll be back up on Thursday night for our usual sojourn. Please be good and keep your thinking clear. You might also use that deep meditation I showed you 2 years ago. REMEM-BER?! ['Remember' is added in black felt pen to the blue ink text.]

I love you Darling and I look forward to sharing with you again.

Lovingly,
Bill

Guilt is its own reward or punishment! [Sentence added in black felt-tip pen.]

I'm certain I wasn't raped down in that furnace room. I don't expect anyone else was, either. I confess all of this now because I want to be free from confusion. I want to be free from fear.

TODAY I RODE BOB'S HORSE

KIM CHINQUEE

I say, "What's with the bow ties?"

They're on his mantel, on his bookshelves, and stuffed pillows in the shape of them are on the sofa. Paintings of bow ties, pictures of him in bow ties. Even some little ones on the necks of his sculptures.

I say, "You must like bow ties."

While Bob cleans up, I look around the house.

I brought the food tonight and drinks. We have mai tais and eat crabs and raw kalettes at his bungalow with its sculptures. Figures of naked bodies.

Bob was riding when I met him. We spent the afternoon riding his horses. Not sure if they're his horses. He says he feeds them every day, brushes them, talks to them, saying he's their boss. He doesn't have a job. Maybe that's his job—horse tending.

I grew up tending cows, leading them in circles. I cleaned them.

Things were messy at my home then: my dad kicking cows, smelling of their shit. My mom said he was the boss with good reason—the same verse she repeated when my dad kicked me.

Bob sips his drink. The lights are low as he pours one more mai tai for me and makes a toast to his first wife, who died, and commends his mistress, who lives in another city.

I FIGURE

KIM CHINQUEE

After he gets up to use the bathroom, I lie on my back, still naked, balancing my wineglass on my stomach, flexing my muscles to try to keep the glass upright. I put my hands in close proximity to the glass, and when it looks like it might tip, I flex some more, picking up the glass when I have to. The wine is white. I figure it's harmless.

I met him online, and after a couple phone calls, we had drinks at a low-lit bistro down the road. He's a surgeon. A recent transplant. He lives across the street from where I used to live until last year, when I moved into my new place.

I used to walk past this building all the time. It was my neighborhood. Every morning and night I'd take my dog out, first with one boyfriend, then another, then another. I lived there for five years, the longest I've lived anywhere.

After this guy elevatored me up to his apartment and I looked out, I saw only the brick of a building I used to see the other side of all the time. His kitchen is smaller than his bathroom.

It's kind of disappointing.

I wonder what he's doing now other than taking off the condom.

When we met, he said he was famous for heart surgery. He showed me his hands. He has pretty fingers. Dark skin and darker circles under his even darker eyes. Thick black hair. Not tall but certainly not short. Muscular. A runner.

I'm a chemist, I had to remind him. I'm decent with equations.

We fucked. I figured it was harmless.

I focus on my abs, on balancing the glass. I flex.

When he comes back, I point to the glass and I say, See?

He says, You're very balanced.

He's naked, his things hanging. He gets in bed again. I watch the glass. I work on balancing. He laughs and says, You're very balanced. He laughs so hard he makes the bed move. I don't think it's funny.

Shut the fuck up, I say. The glass almost tips.

I figure I am harmless.

I HAVE TO FLY

KIM CHINQUEE

I say, My throat is sore, head's like an explosion. I have to fly in two days to present at a conference.

So you're respected? he says.

I hope!

He puts his scope to my chest, my back, looks into my nose, mouth, and eyes. My ears, I say, they've been hurting.

He has certificates on the wall that celebrate his achievements. Today he wears a pressed blue shirt with a loaded, colorful tie.

He says, Likely you'll be okay, but I'll still give you steroids.

So you're very respected? I say.

THE UNIVERSE WOULD BE SO CRUEL

SOUVANKHAM THAMMAVONGSA

Mr. Vong stretched his neck to look over the tops of the heads of the wedding guests, trying to take in a good view of the bride and groom. When he spotted them, he made a bold prediction: "Ah, lovely. Too bad it isn't going to last." Mr. Vong had been invited, not because he was a relative or because he was well acquainted with the parents. He was the one the young couple turned to, being the only printer who offered Lao lettering on wedding invitations. He was highly sought after for his Lao fonts and his eloquence with the language, his knowledge of how little things can shape and affect outcomes. Sure, his clients could download fonts and print them out at Kinko's, but that kind of lazy effort could signify a lazy marriage, one where at the first sign of trouble divorce would be the answer. And anyway, most of his clients didn't know how to write in Lao, having been born here. They needed him to impress their parents.

Mr. Vong took great care, made his own paper, every fiber dried and flattened in his shop, taking several months. He understood more than anyone the superstitions Lao people had about getting names and dates exact throughout the entire process, how a spelling error during the proofing process could foretell an error in marriage, could change the fate of the couple. He regarded himself as the gatekeeper of their good fortune.

Mr. Vong printed their wedding invitations and charged a very small price in hopes that word would get around about his good printing shop. He didn't make much money on his services. Most of his clients were the ones the bigger businesses didn't want to deal with—men and women working for themselves, who didn't buy in bulk, who didn't have much time to be on the Internet, who didn't speak English but somehow, through some signals of hands and sounds, something could be understood about what they wanted. He took the time to talk to each person and spent many hours helping them pick out material and paint. These clients he liked best. They reminded him of himself—farmers coming into his shop with dirty fingernails because they worked out in the field all day, or butchers who didn't have time to change out of clothes stained with blood from a fresh kill. All of them, doing the grunt work of the world.

The clients he didn't like were the salesmen dressed in fine business suits—the ones who always asked for things to be cheaper so they could get a larger cut of the profit. He chased these men away. He spotted them the way you spot danger. The crease of their pressed suits, the leather briefcase, slicked-back hair, perfect English. They called him "buddy," corrected his spelling. It all made him yell, "Fuck you!" Sometimes, when he was in a good mood and had time to spare and felt like humoring them, he would allow them to be in his shop for fifteen minutes, allow them to talk on and on, to show him their graphs. But he'd eventually get back to yelling the same thing he'd yell at the others like them who had come before. The world treated men like this well. They had offices in towers, and secretaries, but in his shop, one he owned and operated alone, he was boss! And he wasn't going to give them the same treatment others had given them. Of course this didn't make much for him in terms of dollars, but that wasn't the point. The point was to be free, to own a thing you had all to yourself, and to be able to say, "Fuck you! All of you all! Fuck you into hell!" Whatever that really meant, Mr. Vong didn't know, but it was fun to say, something that had been said to him at one point. Fun indeed to see these men lose their smooth talk and make their quick, fumbling exits.

Above all, it was the wedding invitations. They were what gave him the most joy in his work.

This wedding couple had anticipated a very high price for Mr. Vong's care and expertise—but it was not at all. They were so happy, they instantly invited him to their wedding, both of them smiling with their even, bright teeth. With teeth that white, that well-cared-for, there was no reason they could not have offered to pay more than he had asked. But instead they accepted the price like those salesmen, eager for the bargain. No marriage would last where two people didn't recognize what would be the right thing to do.

Now, it was at this point in the night—after the guests had been served papaya salad, spring rolls, minced chicken with fresh herbs and spices, sticky rice, and sweets wrapped in banana leaves—when the bride and groom were having their first dance as husband and wife, that Mr. Vong made his bold prediction.

"Ai, why are you saying this for? Keep your voice down!" Mrs. Vong, his devoted and loyal wife of twenty years, urged, slapping him on his arm and looking around at the people seated at their table, wondering if they had heard. It did not appear so, as everyone else seemed to be busying themselves with their food or in their conversations with each other.

"Just you mark my words: Less than a year. That's my prediction. Less than a year." He returned to his meal, gathering up the minced chicken with a flattened ball of sticky rice.

Mr. and Mrs. Vong's daughter listened. She was amused and curious about the accuracy of his prediction. Her father tended to be right about these things.

"Dad, you know for sure?"

"I know. I know these things," he said.

True enough, in less than a year the bride and groom were divorced.

Later that year, Mr. Vong made another one of his predictions. This time he made it the minute he opened the wedding invitation. He said, "Ah, not even going to happen."

The wedding invitation had not been printed by Mr. Vong. One could presume that the prediction was the result of some petty competition or his hurt pride. It was printed at a fancy shop, downtown on a street called Richmond, whose only specialty was printing invitations. There was no Lao lettering to be found anywhere on the invitation. It was fancy and had raised print. The little silver-sparkled bumps could be felt, running a hand across the lettering, forming the names, addresses, dates. And yes, Mr. Vong's prediction came true. The groom married someone else, named Sue. Phone calls were made: Canceled. Called off.

"Dad, seriously, *how did you know?* "

"Look, I know these things. You just can't have a Lao wedding without Lao letters on the invitation. And you have to have your real name in there. Yeah, it's a long name—but that's *your* name. Why would you want to be Sue if it's really Savongnavathakad? Because, you know, the real Sue will end up marrying the guy if it's there in the invitation."

Now, when it was time for Mr. Vong's daughter to get married, he spared no expense. He ordered sparkled paint from Laos, made out of the crushed wings of a rare local insect. The gold specks were real and not artificial—real shine and shimmer for a real marriage. He printed the invitations and put each one out to dry on a metal rack. Four on each rack, a total of four hundred invitations, an even number. He did everything he could possibly do to ensure that his daughter's wedding invitations were perfect and ready to be sent out into the scrutiny of the universe.

But on the day of the wedding, the groom was not there. He was on the coast of France, vacationing with family. "Look, my family has been planning this for a long time," the boy said. "I just couldn't get out of it. So . . . yeah. Sorry, babes." If the boy's parents even knew about the wedding, Mr. Vong didn't know. They had never met. At the time, Mr. Vong thought nothing of it, didn't question, wasn't curious. And now, thinking of it, there was always some excuse and it was always something coming out of that boy's small mouth. It was as if Mr. Vong's plans were of no value, or of lesser value, or not even up for consideration. It didn't occur to him to ask questions. He believed what he was told. There had been a proposal, and that's all he had needed to know about that.

Mr. Vong's daughter threw the phone onto the floor and it stayed complete and solid in its protective case, invented for such situations. Then she ran. She ran and opened the first door she saw, but it turned out to be a closet. She folded herself in there and cried. He let her cry and shooed away everyone who tried to comfort her. A woman ought to cry, he thought. She ought to be allowed to bawl it all out.

And after, she said, "Dad? Dad . . . are you there?"

"Yes. I am right here," he said.

"It's all your fault, isn't it? The invitations . . . something must have gone wrong."

Mr. Vong thought of an answer—one he could use to explain, to reason out what had happened to the day—how the wedding had come to this. "I . . . I found one invitation behind the door." He talked to his daughter as if he were a small school-boy who had stolen an eraser to win the affections of his friend, and had now been summoned by the head master to explain. "I must have missed it. The one. All invitations must go out. It was just one. I didn't know the universe would be so cruel. I am terribly sorry. I am trained to know, to predict, and to ensure these things." It was not true at all, of course. He had accounted for everything! But this was no time for his own pride. No amount of *fuck-you-to-hell*s could make a difference to that boy. How could you tell her that the boy wasn't kind or good, that she wasn't loved by that boy, that sometimes what felt like love only *felt* like love, and wasn't real? And that even if it had been real, sometimes love can stop spinning like a top you set in motion. You couldn't do anything about that, but, you could say, *Yes, yes, an invitation fell behind the door. That's what it was.*

TALE OF THE TRIBE

TETMAN CALLIS

All parties involved, including the second Dan and the second Suzanne in the distant city, ceased fucking each other and moved on to fuck others who were once upon a time of some consequence.

But still the first Dan and the first Suzanne continued not to fuck.

The second Dan came to stay with the first Steve. Though the first Suzanne had removed herself from the premises, she was still near enough to fuck. She and the second Dan so commenced.

In yet another distant city, there had been throughout this time yet another Suzanne and another Steve. They also, of course, fucked, and of course they also came to cease their fucking and to go their separate ways and to fuck others. The third Suzanne, in her fashion, headed to the city where the first Suzanne and the second Dan had likewise recently ceased their fucking.

These people!

Meanwhile, the first Dan and the first Suzanne continued not to fuck.

The first and third Suzannes met at an event. Hi, my name is Suzanne. Oh, what a coincidence, my name is Suzanne, too.

Later, they smoked cigarettes and told their stories, including one in which a Stephanie was mentioned.

PLEASE

KATHRYN SCANLAN

I went alone to the pagan museum and to the historic fountain because he'd been unable to defecate since we'd arrived, nearly a week prior. When I returned at dinnertime he held a baguette in one hand and a length of salami in the other, tearing a bite from each before speaking. I can force it out this way, he said.

His face was very red and he was sweating but I washed a glass and poured him a beer and we sat on the terrace drinking until it was time to lie down—though the regular residents of that place were just waking up.

He rejected medicine of any kind—believed in the body and its mechanisms. He competed regularly in prolonged events of strenuous activity, and could lift me off the ground with one hand in his pocket.

Nonetheless, when I awoke, he'd bound himself in the bedsheets and he was breathing in a heavy, smacking way.

I prepared the coffee and on a small plate arranged carefully washed fruits. Soon he set his cup down, sloshing the coffee over the rim in his excitement, and hurried to the bathroom.

He picked up the cup from its puddle when he came out and shook his head sadly—though by then the coffee had gone cold, and he would not drink cold coffee.

I might have envied his predicament, since whatever I swallowed made its swift and irritable trip from one end to the other, resulting in daily harassment. In a similar manner, I rush from one situation to the next, often arriving too quickly.

Yet I could sit in a restaurant and request of the waiter some water and plain vegetables, please, and be understood. A little heap of the vegetables on a plate would arrive a few minutes later—lightly steamed, steaming still—accompanied by a small cup of oil or melted butter for dipping or drizzling, though most often I ate them unadorned between sips of water.

I went on to collect pamphlets and paused to read plaques of note. In one plaza people had been bound and set alight— alive—by their fellow citizens. In another, shoppers had been trampled by a large herd of animals.

Later, at the entrance to a park, I stood before a pair of pillars topped with a pair of heads—a man's and a woman's whose noses had been chipped to snubs—and on the woman's crown of cold braids was a pigeon, releasing from its undercarriage a loose white drib that slid down the woman's cheek like a teardrop.

. . .

Back at the apartment, I found him slumped in a chair—pasty and waxen—and not wishing to talk.

Could I walk without toppling? Would I make it in time to relieve myself?

How funny—how funny—the baring of ass—how good to sit.

There then came an angry banging on the door. But it was the hot hiss I was listening to, the miraculous stream—unaided, unbeckoned—of what had so recently been lolling around in my mouth.

When at last I opened the door, he was standing right there, as if roused from a spell. A clump—oily and black—was on the floor.

I made it, he said—casting a proud look down upon it and upon me—and for dinner I'll have some soft yellow cheese.

HA! I SAID QUIETLY

AMANDA GOLDBLATT

In the pool I at last had a cap. It had arrived by mail the day prior. My hair, against my efforts, had been hollowing its follicles in repeated exposure to chlorine. The cap fit on my head like a balloon fits on a head: not well. As I pushed deep from the wall I found my head was buoyant. There was air trapped in my cap. I found I had to use my head as a sort of driver, with increased downward effort, which I imagined was splitting not only the water but the great, ineffable stuff of the planet: a cosmos or whatever.

There was a man whom I saw once a week at the indoor pool despite going there three to four times each week. He was relatively fit and had tattoos, a beard, and a haircut similar to the haircuts of many other men in the neighborhood. There were other people whom I regularly saw at the pool, but he was the only one I was interested in racing against. I beat him every time, lapped him even when using a kickboard, relying only on my legs, which were—let's admit it—my strongest parts. He of course was ignorant of our competition, and, when he emerged from the men's locker room back into the pool area, in order to exit, he was put-together in a casual-professional outfit with contemporary detailing and materials. In other words: no matter how often I beat him, he always won.

As one winter month was defeated by the next, I learned to wear my swim cap in a way so it did not catch air. As a result of this, I returned to a state of sleekness, and swam even faster than before. It was easy to imagine myself as a marine animal. The chlorinated water tasted bitter in a pleasant way.

That morning at the pool, the tattooed man was already swimming. I found it funny that I could neither describe nor enumerate the tattoos despite seeing this man weekly for so long. "Ha!" I said quietly.

I went to the women's locker room, where it smelled like human shit, as it sometimes did, especially after the children's classes, which were held twice a week in the midmorning. I suspected someone was leaving diapers in the locker room trash. However, it was the morning lap session, prior to the mid-morning classes, and so there was no explanation. The tattooed man and I had not ever met during a morning session. Or really, strictly: we had not ever met.

The tattooed man paddle-handed a poor crawl across the water. The teenage lifeguards yawned like cats, draping themselves around the front counter, and smiled in my direction. I walked to the deep end. I took a plumb jump down in.

I let my force take me twelve feet down and my buoyancy take me all the way back up. I pushed off from the wall and moved half the length of the pool beneath the surface. As I rose, my cap filled with air. After nineteen smooth strokes and two breaths, I was at the other side, patting my head and pulling at the silicone rubber. As I did so, the tattooed man approached the wall. Usually he swam continuously for approximately thirty minutes. When he met the wall, his hands cupped the lip for a moment before he was off again.

Because it was morning still, and the pool was heated poorly, slowly, to approximately sixty-eight degrees year-round, my teeth chattered. Sixty-eight degrees is ideal only on land. I myself felt cold and fine. My strokes were even smoother than usual, and my cap more obedient than it had been, and I cut through the chalk-tasting, clear, cold water, imagining I was escaping something. I did my usual thirty laps, and then another fifteen. I was, at last, free.

When I got out of the pool the tattooed man was dressed and standing on the pool deck. As I passed him he said, "You have an admirable stroke." I nodded so he would know I had heard him.

After showering, rinsing my suit and cap, and dressing carefully in up to three layers on each extremity, I left the locker room. The shit smell had, during my swim, been cut through with bleach. This satisfied me, though the aftereffect odor was imperfect. The tattooed man was standing beside the building's flagpole, on which no flag flew. It was only slowly that it became clear he was waiting for me, as he did not move or flinch as I drew closer but, rather, turned his face toward me and began to advance.

I was unused to being advanced upon, in my usually un-peopled life. Because of this, I found that the man's movements increased my heart rate. The man wore a neatly tied scarf, knotted like an ascot or something similar. "Tut-tut," he said to me. I wondered if he was one of those "Anglophiles." Or merely one of those stylish residents of our up-and-coming neighborhood who are able to select several affectations from across cultural traditions with neither self-consciousness nor worry, or with the "correct" amount of self-consciousness and worry. I said hello. He seemed, via micro-movements of his eyebrows and lips, pleased by my acknowledgement. The man asked if I would like to get some coffee.

I asked the tatooed man if the men's locker room ever smelled like human shit. Flaring his nostrils, he asked again if I would like to join him for coffee. With keen amusement I watched a single, clumsy pigeon launch itself up into the white sky. He nodded slightly and then walked away, permitting me to do the same.

That night I slept and did not dream, as I did not usually dream, or I did not usually remember dreaming. It was something to do with the way I slept: in small sections, a lap at a time. It was not uncommon for me to rise from bed to look out the window at the streets of the city. The darkened view made me calm and joyful.

One day there were only women swimming laps. We came in many shapes and ages. I wondered where the tattooed man or any man was. I thought about how I didn't care if I beat any of the women but perhaps I was lying to myself. As I left the bleach-smelling warmth of the locker room, so did another swimmer. "You're speedy!" she shouted at me. I found that I reviled her. We walked side by side across the deck and into the world. A blizzard-like snow began to fall, both wet and sharp, and I had the feeling the weather was struggling to be something.

PAINTINGS

GENIEVE FIGGIS

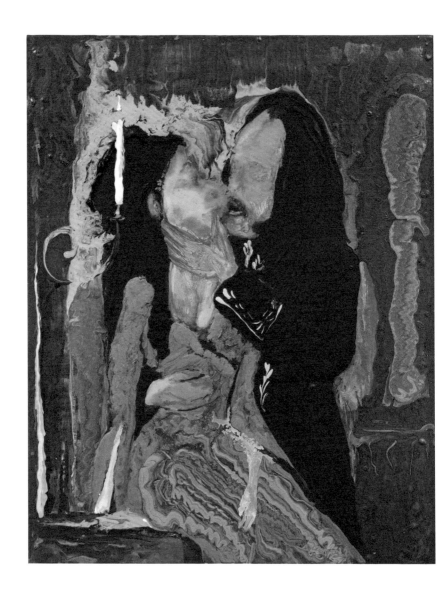

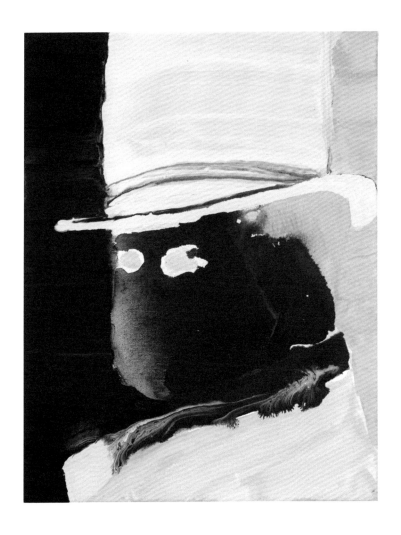

(Images have been provided courtesy of the artist
and Half Gallery, New York.)

IN A SEXUAL SLANG

VI KHI NAO

This morning I woke up with a bladder full of magnets and petroleum. Parts of me are magnetized to heliotrope, which refers to heliotropium, and made me think of floral petroleum. The other parts of me are craving an extremely sanitized asshole and a microphone. Centuries ago, the ancients wouldn't have guessed that the human asshole can be used as a hydrocarbon pipeline. This, and getting blown up from the inside and becoming a half-mourning periorbital flower, not from war, but from peace. When the petroleum left my body somebody once compared the departure to an Ethiopian exodus. I find myself walking slowly in a sexual slang toward the Gaza Strip. A woman who pinned my soul down told me I could pull a sofa over near where the sea wept and sip *qamar deen* and I could taste the entire

Koran that way for sure. Sitting in that living room, all the Palestinians smell like chicken broth. Now that my body is no longer a prisoner of gas pipes, my stomach can be a pillowcase filled with unsalted goat cheese. Later I will talk to my even-toed, wild Bactrian ungulate named Hummus bi Tahini. He has a beautiful asshole. I had him imported from the Gobi desert. We survived several sandstorms together before Saudi Arabia inserted one gas pipeline through my asshole. One friend asked me if I was a gas station.

A BLANKET

VI KHI NAO

Berlin and I have had to inhale the desert whose arms and legs lengthen as we walk. We have not been walking long, and dry sand leaks from the bottoms of our feet while the air surrounds us like confessional knives. Behind or above us, Jerusalem or America. Not long ago, and then, my lungs, Berlin said, are heavy with dark fluids and I don't know if I have the energy to cross the sea of sand with you, Mansion. And I think it's dark, this bed full of waterless air that blooms while Berlin's dry mouth opens behind the Judean hills. We walk slowly, Berlin. One foot over the other foot. I am sorry our faces are peeling off, Berlin. We are only tiny tangerines. Berlin's curly hair flops back onto the mattress of sand. The days pass like the pages of the past. The wind arrives with dehydrating tasks and sometimes Berlin's skirt lives outside of

Jerusalem and has to walk back to Berlin's body, and Mansion's blouse travels like an uncle through a clan of nomads. It's so hard, you know, Mansion, when darkness presses on your skin while the shirt you wear won't iron your soul. You know it's hard to walk away from the Holy City with bags of sand bundled like newborn calves beneath my calves. I want to tell Berlin that we do not have to be Moses and talk to God and we do not have to kill an Egyptian and hide him in the sand. Our task is very simple . . . all we are obliged and destined to do is to lift this one page made of miles and miles of biblical eyes and mouths off the Holy desert and see what lies beneath. Not too far from us, the windless wind turns the pages of Berlin's bible like a switchblade. Berlin delivers her words: Mansion, I wish we brought our banana leaf sleeping bags with us. I wish that, too, Berlin. I wish we were sleeping beneath a banana tree and in my sleep I would make you a sleeping bag from the arms of the banana tree.

IS THAT OKAY WITH ME?

VI KHI NAO

The moaning comes from a small hut in a British bush by a woman spreading wide for a man and later wider for a woman. My cunt turns around in reluctance and walks quietly into a field of pubic hair and a field of amputated hands. You are sprawled out, vulnerable to my finger that runs along your English skin, a partition between the Assad milieu and your river of red hemoglobin. Above, the sun keeps on rising while the eastern border whimpers a little, a little into the skin of fog. You said that you would dye your hair blond for me so that when I fucked you, it would seem as if I were yanking the sun out of you.

I ASK THE SENTENCE

VI KHI NAO

I ask the sentence to move across the carpet floor.

I ask it not to drag its paragraphical legs while doing so.

I ask it not to be lonely, not to have ethical issues with women with menstrual cramps, or periods, and whatnot.

I ask the sentence to conduct itself in a way that does not deny the social conditions of other sentences, that does not make any sentence feel left out or suicidal.

I ask the sentence to be chivalrous, to open semantic doors for women, and not to treat children as linguistic concubines for imperial expansion.

I ask the sentence not to open fire on any other sentence.

I ask the sentence to be self-reliant, to use itself as a mirror for narcissistic reasons and not to ask other sentences for monetary support.

I ask the sentence not to hypnotize other sentences, so that they don't become organ donors to objects, nouns, pronouns, and indirect objects.

I ask the sentence not to be an alcoholic, not to inebriate streams of consciousness, the passive voice, C. D. Wright.

I ask the sentence to be reasonable in a Haitian ransom note, just five more sentences, just five more sentences and I will let your mother, the paragraph, go.

I ask the sentence not to leave her semicolon inside a hot van in the middle of the summer and to leave the Budapest train station, but never to walk 105 miles to the border of Austria.

I ask the sentence not to write that sentence; you know that sentence, the one where it has too much hypermasculinity in it, the one with the toilet lid up, you know that one.

I ask the sentence to please, to please marry Gary Lutz.

I LIKED HER

RACHELE RYAN

I called her J, after the packs of Jay Arthur cigarettes she left around her apartment. J had biggish cheeks and flat gray eyes and a tall, squishy body with freckled skin. She wasn't pretty, but I guess I'd say I liked her teeth. They were irregular and small, tiny white bits pressed up into pink gums. I could imagine their feel. Her hair was cut in those little baby bangs, real close to the hairline. I watched her trim them once with nail scissors above a trash can in her kitchen, the blades going *zzzp-zzzp* every time they shut. She lived in Alphabet City, above a pharmacy with a buzzing fluorescent sign that lit the whole place up red. Something about that red made her movements strange, like an old reel of film with some of its frames missing.

Last night she lay with her mouth open. There is no window

in the room, but the red light filters in from the hallway and I could make out her shape, legs straight, arms at her sides. She slept in that way where her lids closed only a little and the whites of her eyeballs showed.

I knelt at her bedside while she looked at me in her sleep. I stood up again and removed my trousers, and then stretched out along her side. I moved my hand over the panels of her face, and slipped my thumb between her lips. Her tongue, wet and alive, swelled, and I played with the thin bit of skin at its base. She choked a little. I waited, but she did not move again. I removed my thumb and put my mouth over her mouth. Then I placed my hand across her face, after that. Using my other arm, I pushed her legs apart, slowly. They were heavier than I would have thought, but I did all right. I held her there. In the middle of it, her eyes opened. Her pupils shrank, then expanded, then shrank. A noise came out from under my hand, deflated.

When I was done I put my trousers back on and stood for a moment above her bed. She didn't even move a hand. Her lips came apart as though she were about to say something, but when nothing came out she brought them together again.

I guessed she might like a glass of water, so I went into the kitchen to get one for her. I held the glass under the faucet until it was full, and then I let the water run over onto my hand. It took a while for the water to cool. Outside the air was filmy. I saw a cat, a skinny thing, run between the trash cans at the base of the building. It kept pawing at this banana peel. I figured it might want something more substantial, so I took the milk from the fridge and poured it out the window. It went down in a long, wiggly stream, and ran all over the pavement.

THE REST OF IT

NATHAN DRAGON

Danny's digging a hole. He's been digging it for a little bit now. Danny's retired but his wife, Margaret, still works. He could not dig without her. Danny used to work in a small restaurant in town until he could not work there anymore. Before Danny started digging, he used to do all of the laundry and he used to make sure the clothesline was taut and he used to work at that restaurant. Danny had done enough he thinks. People ask him,

"Danny, whatcha doin, bawd?"

"Digging," Danny says.

"Whatcha diggin' for?"

"Well, we'll find out."

"Eh Danny, why you diggin'?"

"I've done the rest of it," Danny says, waving his trowel.

KATHY JANCO SITTING ON A PENCIL

SUSAN LAIER

Kathy Janco sat on a pencil in fourth grade. The pencil penetrated her left butt cheek.

All the other little girls were embarrassed for her when the principal and the nurse had to look at the pencil in her butt, down in the main office. Some of the boys laughed and made jokes— all of it was great preparation for what happened to her later.

SILLY

SUSAN LAIER

Susan Ellen outsold every other salesperson and it was her first job as an adult and she was a champion, an ace. Her list of items sold was always longer than anyone else's and usually ran both sides of an ordinary piece of paper. The idea was to make ALL the sales—to keep smiling, talking, having fun while directing each lady toward the idea of looking great during her vacation on the Cape.

One afternoon, after 155 customers and 150 sales, Susan Ellen was talking silly but still selling. She was a little too rambling of the mouth.

A pretty but chubby lady came in to get dressed up for a night on the town. She kept trying on one thing after another.

Nothing fit. Finally, as she pushed her roll into a pair of jeans that wouldn't zip, Susan Ellen said, "You're just too fat!"

The insulted customer ran out of the store. So Susan Ellen was still talking silly, but not selling.

EVERYONE LIKED HIM

SUSAN LAIER

There was something different about the teacher named Mr. Russell. We children did not know exactly what that could be, but he surely acted more like a girl than a guy. He was kind and nice enough as a teacher. Sometimes he was the bus monitor, standing there while students got on and off, arriving or heading home. Four or five times a day, there he was, Mr. Russell, directing the funny little children on and off the buses. One day a blond little boy with a brush cut handed him a note. Mr. Russell said before he read it, "Oh, a note for me? How tender."

WHAT THE VACUUM CLEANER DID

SUSAN LAIER

John gives Jaz an engagement ring. It cost $6000. It is made of diamonds and one big emerald. John has a car transport business and makes lots of money.

John and Jaz fight too much. Jaz sucks up the engagement ring in the vacuum cleaner to hide it in case John demands that Jaz return it, which he does. Jaz says she does not know where the ring is. John has fits searching for the ring and he even shakes out the vacuum-cleaner dirt bag, knowing somehow it can only be in there. He gets no results and gives up and finally goes away somewhere.

Jaz is puzzled but carefully checks the dirt bag. Yes, the ring falls out and pings onto the floor. She retrieves it before it rolls down the heater grate nearby. She moves out of John's house and sells the ring for $1500.

FALLING ON THE FLOOR LAUGHING

SUSAN LAIER

I shared a special reading class with Ronnie when he was in the fourth grade and I was in the third. Once our reading teacher asked us if we could make up any amazing story, what would it be? And Ronnie said he'd like to make up a tragic comedy. "What's that?" asked our teacher. Ronnie answered, "Someone could die laughing." Which it seems he started to do. He laughed so hard when he came out with that one that he fell off the chair, twisted up his legs, and folded himself on the floor like a carpenter's wooden ruler. At that moment, it was easy to understand why he had been diagnosed with a "nervous stomach" and had to eat crackers and milk in the middle of every morning during arithmetic.

HE WOULD HAVE TO TOUCH HER

ASHTON POLITANOFF

He locked the door and lifted the toilet seat with the tip of his shoe. Midstream, he heard her try the knob.

It's locked, he said.

When he opened she was there. He angled past so as not to touch her and sat down on the couch as if he were trying it out in a store. She straightened a crooked lampshade and smiled at him.

He stood up and checked under the cushions of the couch.

Did you lose something? she asked.

He removed one cushion and then the other. He found what he was looking for. He pulled out the bed and set the legs down gently. It had its own sheets already. All it needed was a pillow.

How many pillows does the bed have? he asked. How many? he asked again, but she wouldn't answer.

She came over and with a flat palm she pressed just below his belt buckle.

He searched for a swelling of some kind, an indication of how to proceed. He looked down his own nose and waited for it.

BOBBY CIGARETTE

GREG MULCAHY

He picked a fight with himself, and it did not go well.

He wanted some language—something with comfort and wealth.

Who would not?

Instead he built his shrine to Loser Town. Threw everything at it. Things he could not love. Things he could not be.

HIS LIFE WAS STEADY

ROBERT TINDALL

Any love was one part of the question when the spring weather arrived and it was very nice and Brenlan had taken a good look at himself.

His years in middle age did follow a chemical truth—the idea that maybe the strife was over with—the waiting was done—and optimism came next.

His life was steady even though Brenlan was leading a secret life in a rented room in Wisconsin—and although he was vile about some things in his mind—he did very well understand—he had love and he had umbrage and he had a fine time. He drank soda pop and he smoked and he rode the bus here and there—he would later encounter some difficulty but he had straightened up to fly right.

A danger did obtain only sometimes. It was so very good it seemed the city of Chicago was at his feet—he was sober and he knew an exciting hour now and then and it was as if he knew a certain success.

The real problem one day seemed to be the mischief of any average woman and a fear would arise later.

The doctor was a tall man and he talked on a telephone—Brenlan sat in the lobby of the administration building at the hospital, in the north of the state of Georgia where he had traveled, mildly pleased by the pressure of being alone. He was happily focused on his own future.

Maybe he would narrowly survive his own foolishness.

When Brenlan got back it was quiet and he had half the problem solved—a new lock device with a paper card to enter the room at the motel whether he liked it or not. See he had been to this motel a dozen times or more. It proved to him that half of his so-called problem was about money and about how hard it was to come by—but the place was comfortable and was something charming—he learned this pouring himself a coffee in the rental office.

The women—it seemed bright to see them—he wondered if they would last on into the future even though they were of a mold to seem something dull or foreign, either—the old men sat at a table with something noble in their pasts.

He visited his home and to be sure it was very nice. His memory was spotty and he had learned that. He found himself to be growing old.

Later he would recall the memory of the store only it was a memory tainted by doubt in general whether he would have to change or at least take a look at such a handy fact that the sales-women in the shops were implacable and that they knew all the hidden doings of their customers.

He was happy to cite his halcyon years now that they were done. See life was good and the resentment did ebb when he caught a bus for the city and he had taken care of his mind that way.

CONTRIBUTORS

Tetman Callis is a frequent contributor to *NOON*. His fictions have also appeared in *New York Tyrant*, *Salt Hill*, *New Orleans Review*, and *Identity Theory*, among other publications. He is the author of *High Street: Lawyers, Guns & Money in a Stoner's New Mexico* and *Franny & Toby*. He lives in Chicago.

Kim Chinquee is the author of the collections *Oh Baby*, *Pretty*, and *Pistol*. Her collection *Milk* is forthcoming in 2017 from Ravenna Press and she recently finished a novel, *A Zillion Pirouettes*, based on her experiences during the Boston bombings. She is senior editor of *New World Writing*. This is her sixteenth appearance in *NOON*. She lives in Buffalo, New York.

Lydia Davis's latest book of stories is *Can't and Won't*. Her most recent translations are, from the Dutch, *Hurt to the Bone: Very Short Stories* by A. L. Snijders (AFdH, 2016) and, from the French, *Fibrils*, the third volume of Michel Leiris's autobiographical essay, *Rules of the Game* (Yale University Press, forthcoming in 2017), and a collection of Marcel Proust's letters to his upstairs neighbor (New Directions, forthcoming in 2017).

Nathan Dragon lives in Chicago. "The Rest of It" is Dragon's first appearance in *NOON* and his first published story.

Lucie Elven lives in Brooklyn, New York. This is her second appearance in *NOON*.

Genieve Figgis's first solo exhibition in New York was at Half Gallery, New York in 2014 followed by a solo exhibition at Almine Rech Gallery in London in 2015. Her first book, *Making Love with the Devil*, was published by Fulton Ryder in 2014, and her work has been reviewed in *The New York Times*, *ARTnews*, *Vice*, *Artsy*, *GQ*, *W Magazine*, *Vanity Fair*, and *Artforum*, among other publications. Recently, she collaborated with the Metropolitan Opera to create an animated film, set to Gaetano Donizetti's *Roberto Devereux*, for the Gallery Met Shorts series. Figgis is currently based in County Wicklow, Ireland.

Amanda Goldblatt's work has appeared in *The Southern Review*, *Fence*, *American Short Fiction*, and elsewhere. She lives in Chicago. This is her first appearance in *NOON*.

Augusta Gross is a frequent contributor to *NOON*. She composes music for piano and wind instruments; her most recent album is *Below Sea Level*. She has just completed a piece for clarinet and piano commissioned by clarinetist Seunghee Lee.

Brandon Hobson is a regular contributor to *NOON*. His work has also appeared in *Conjunctions*, *Post Road*, *The Believer*, *The Paris Review Daily*, and elsewhere. His story "Past the EconoLodge," from *NOON* 2014, won a 2016 Pushcart Prize.

Vi Khi Nao is the author of the poetry collection *The Old Philosopher*, winner of 2014 Nightboat Poetry Prize. Her manuscript *A Brief Alphabet of Torture* won the FC2 2016 Ronald Sukenick Innovative Fiction Contest. In fall 2016, Coffee House Press will publish her novel, *Fish in Exile*.

Susan Laier is a poet and fiction writer. She also paints and is a master leatherworker. She lives in Waterford, New York. This is her third appearance in *NOON*.

Clancy Martin is a writer and philosophy professor. He lives in Kansas City, Missouri. He is a frequent contributor to *NOON*.

Greg Mulcahy is the author of *Out of Work*, *Constellation*, *Carbine*, and *O'Hearn*. He lives in Minnesota. He is a frequent contributor to *NOON*.

Jana Paleckova is a self-taught artist living in the Czech Republic. She is represented in the United States by the Fred Giampietro Gallery in New Haven, Connecticut. She had her first major exhibition in New York City at the 2016 Outsider Art Fair.

Ashton Politanoff is frequent contributor to *NOON*. He lives in Redondo Beach, California.

Rachele Ryan lives in Portland, Maine. This is her first appearance in *NOON*.

Kathryn Scanlan's work has appeared in *Fence*, *American Short Fiction*, *The Collagist*, *DIAGRAM*, *The Iowa Review*, and *Two Serious Ladies*. She lives in Los Angeles and is a frequent contributor to *NOON*.

Christine Schutt's most recent novel is *Prosperous Friends*. She is the author of two other novels, *Florida* and *All Souls*, and two collections of stories, *Nightwork* and *A Day, a Night, Another Day, Summer*.

Walter Serner (1889–1942) was born Walter Eduard Seligmann in Karlsbad, Bohemia (now part of the Czech Republic). He was a German-language journalist, essayist, and fiction writer eventually associated with the Swiss Dada movement. The second part of his *Letzte Lockerung: Ein Handbrevier für Hochstapler und solche, die es werden wollen*, from which the work in this present edition of *NOON* was taken, was written in 1927 and consists of 590 tongue-in-cheek numbered instructions or precepts, grouped into 13 titled sections. In 1933, his books were banned by the Nazi government, and in 1942, he and his wife were deported from Prague to Terezin and thence to Minsk or Riga, where they were most likely shot. The complete work will appear next year in Mark Kanak's translation from Twisted Spoon Press in Prague.

Rhoads Stevens is frequent contributor to *NOON*. He lives in Seattle.

Souvankham Thammavongsa is a Canadian poet and fiction writer. Two of her stories were included in *The Journey Prize Stories* 28: *The Best of Canada's New Writers* (Penguin Random House Canada, 2016). This is her second appearance in *NOON*. She is studying to become an accountant.

Robert Tindall is a frequent contributor to *NOON*. He lives in Evanston, Illinois.

Rob Walsh is the author of *Troublers*, a collection of stories. His work has appeared in previous editions of *NOON*.

Mika Yamamoto has work published and forthcoming in *Nimrod International Journal*, *Palo Alto Review*, *Foliate Oak*, *The Rumpus*, *The Writer's Chronicle*, and elsewhere. Her fiction was previously published in *NOON* 2009. She lives in Midland, Michigan.

THE EDITORS WISH TO THANK THE FOLLOWING
INDIVIDUALS FOR THEIR GENEROUS SUPPORT OF NOON:

Eleanor Alper
Katie Baldwin
The Balsamo Family Foundation
Margaret Barrett
Francis and Prudence Beidler
Marcy Brownson and Edwin J. Wesely
Melinda Davis and Ealan Wingate
Lawrie and Tony Dean
Eugen Friedlaender Foundation
Nancy Evans
Joseph Glossberg
Lisa Grunwald
Mark Hage
Diane Holsenbeck
Ellen Kern
Christina Kirk
Laura S. Kirk
Lucy Kissel
Lucy and Kenneth Lehman
Shoshanna Lonstein
Joyce Lowinson
Ruth and Irving Malin
Clancy Martin
Pam Michaelcheck
Wolfgang Neumann
Melanie Niemiec
Nuveen Investments
Szilvia Szmuk-Tanenbaum
Lisa Taylor
Lily Tuck
Abby S. Weintraub
Paul C. Williams
Anonymous (2)

A NOTE ON THE TYPE

This book was set in Fournier, a typeface named for Pierre Simon Fournier, a celebrated type designer in eighteenth-century France. Fournier's type is considered transitional in that it drew its inspiration from the old style yet was ingeniously innovative, providing for an elegant yet legible appearance. For some time after his death, in 1768, Fournier was remembered primarily as the author of a famous manual of typography and as a pioneer of the print system. However, in 1925 his reputation was enhanced when the Monotype Corporation of London revived Fournier's roman and italic.

Typeset by Bessas & Ackerman
Printed by GHP, West Haven, Connecticut
Cover design by Susan Carroll
NOON is printed on recycled paper
with environmentally friendly inks.

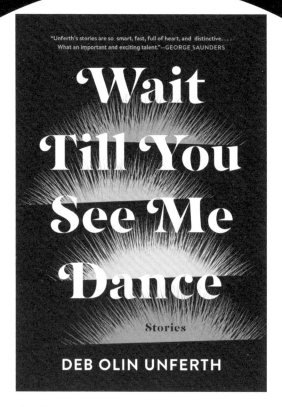

Milk

Short Fictions

Kim
Chinquee

Delivered Fresh!

from Ravenna Press, Spring 2017

MR

3 nobel prize winning authors
14 pulitzer prize winning authors
0 wolf fatalities

for contest details check out www.mississippireview.com

the IOWA REVIEW

IOWAREVIEW.ORG
stories, poems, essays
spring, fall, winter

THE WHITE REVIEW is a quarterly journal featuring fiction, poetry, reportage, essays and artwork, alongside interviews with writers and artists.

MARCEL PROUST

LETTERS TO MY NEIGHBOR

TRANSLATED WITH AN INTRODUCTION BY
LYDIA DAVIS

"Couldn't I send you some books. Tell me what would distract you, I would be so pleased. Don't speak of annoying neighbors, but of neighbors so charming (an association of words contradictory in principle since Montesquiou claims that most horrible of all are 1) neighbors 2) the smell of post offices) that they leave the constant tantalizing regret that one cannot take advantage of their neighborliness."

Summer 2017
New Directions
Independent since 1936
ndbooks.com